BANKSY LOCATIONS & TOURS

By Martin Bull

D0526197

Second Edition

25 locations updated
12 photos improved
several new inset photos
extra love & peace included

Published by shellshock publishing
Second Edition
Copyright © Martin Bull 2007

ISBN 978-0-9554712-1-6

Printed by CPI Bath
Print management by TU ink
www.tuink.co.uk

The author asserts his moral right to be identified as the author of this work.

The author also has dressed up in women's clothes, slept in a hedge and fallen in love with a sheep, and probably doesn't wish to be identified for any of those.

THE BIG ISSUE FOUNDATION

My website is dedicated to Les, a Big Issue seller I met in Bristol.

For copies sold via the author, 20% of his sale price will be donated to The Big Issue Foundation (registered charity no. 1049077). For copies sold via bookshops 10% of the author's sale price of this book will be donated.

100% of sales of a limited edition version of this book is being donated to them.

The Big Issue Foundation does amazing work to assist homeless people, enabling them to gain control of their lives and achieve greater self-reliance and independence.

Please visit - www.bigissue.co.uk/foundation.html

INTRODUCTION

Do you fancy wandering the streets of London looking for graffiti, especially that from Bristol's finest son, Banksy? Or do you prefer just sitting at home in your comfy chair (slippers and pipe optional, but highly recommended in these days of weapons of mass destruction...), looking at photos of his street work and reading a bit about them?

This unique book lets you do either.

Follow my street tours or make your own DIY tour. Collect all the locations like a geek (each location is numbered), or just wander around a bit, stop at pubs, have a fag, and hope to cop a glance into a strip joint (as one tour member proudly told me they had). Or just flick through the book whilst on the crapper. It's all up to you.

The book takes you through 3 tours of Banksy graffiti in London, tells you where each piece is (including postcodes and approximate map/GPS references!), what they look like, a bit of history, some of my photos, the current status of the graffiti (as of about February 2007), and odd mentions of local landmarks such as pubs, markets and tattoo joints.

Don't expect pseudo-intellectual ramblings in this book on what this graffiti all means, how the Banksy phenomenon has taken off, who he is, who he isn't, why my grandmother looks a bit like Arsene Wenger, or what the difference is between graffiti and street art. I'm not that interested in intellectualising all this.

I'll let you decide what it means to you.

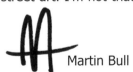
Martin Bull

THE GEEKY BIT

Throughout 2006 many people responded to my leading questions and downright Miss Marpleesque annoyance of where to find a lot of this graffiti / street art. I have also discovered a lot myself whilst wandering the streets like a stray dog, following hunches and leads, and smelling the odd lamp-post to get that authentic feel.

In an effort to share this info and to let people take their own photos (if they want to - it's not compulsory....) I have added the locations of a lot of graffiti (mainly by Banksy and Eine) to two location maps, and in 2006 also arranged and ran a series of free guided tours.

If you want to find all this stuff yourself, there is a free map of Banksy (and other) street art, which I have contributed a lot to. Visit the map at:
www.zeesource.net/maps/map.do?group=1571

There is also an Eine Location Map, which I started and organise - access is free.
Visit the map at - www.zeesource.net/maps/map.do?group=6502

I don't plan to do anymore guided tours until Spring 2007. I don't think it would be too much fun in the winter, with the less favourable weather and worsening light. When I do decide on more, I will always try to advertise the tours and any future books or maps on:

The Banksy ebay forum - http://groups.ebay.co.uk/forum.jspa?forumID=300003968
The Flickr Banksy group - www.flickr.com/groups/banksy/
And my website - www.shellshockphotos.co.uk

HOXTON & SHOREDITCH TOUR

Pages 9 to 81 - Locations S1 to S31

FARRINGDON & CLERKENWELL TOUR

Pages 82 to 119 - Locations F1 to F14

WATERLOO, SOUTH BANK & VICTORIA EMBANKMENT TOUR

Pages 120 to 163 - Locations R1 to R19

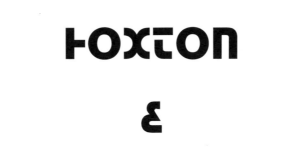

HOXTON

&

SHOREDITCH

TOUR

The biggest tour by far. At a pretty decent pace this took us 3 hours. It could be far more if you include all the local streets and all the local graffiti. It is everywhere. And it's ever changing, so even if some of this has gone by the time of your wanderings, you're bound to always find something new, or even something you never noticed before.

Literally stumbling across 'the maid' (see S19) early-ish one Sunday morning in May (I suspect Banksy did it in the small hours of that Sunday morning) is a pleasure you can only really get by wandering around, keeping your eyes open, and following your destiny (you will be amazed at how many weird situations have led me to come across this stuff!).

This tour goes around the capital of UK street graffiti - Hoxton, Old Street, Shoreditch, and Brick Lane - the creative, yet run-down, neuvo trendy East End. The streets (and railway bridges and skanky alleys) are literally awash with graffiti of all styles, plus paste-ups, stickers, installations, art projects and all sorts of weird and wonderfully creative ramblings (picture frames on the street, nailed up art, tattooists, photographers, fashion victims and maybe Nathan Barley on his poxy BMX if you are unlucky enough).

This tour is the longest of the three, but you could easily split the tour up, or just wander around a bit instead. It's all relatively flat and as it doesn't involve any non-avoidable steps I would have thought that it could be done by someone using a wheelchair or a baby buggy.

You won't need a tube / bus / whatever ticket for this... It's just a lot of walking. When I did it as a tour it took us 3 hours for the full tour.

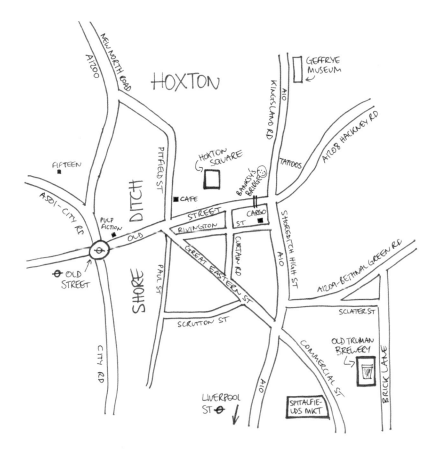

Post Code - EC1Y 1AU
Map / GPS reference - TQ 32796 82288

Location
Oliver's Yard, just off City Rd (A501)

As seen in the Banksy books. It is now fading but it is the only Toxic Rat left in the area, and is complete with green waste spewing across the pavement and the word 'Wanksy' added to it!.

Status
Faded, but clearly visible.

Next
Return to Old St station and use the subways to come out at Exit 8.

S1

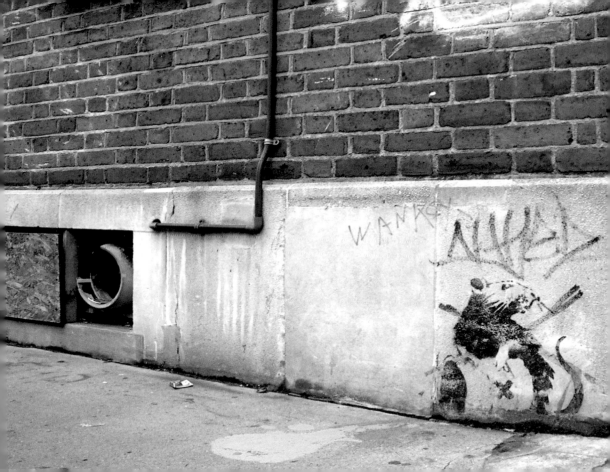

CHECK OUT THE WALL

Post Code - EC1V 2NR
Map / GPS reference - TQ 32706 82522

Location
By Exit 8 of Old Street Tube station

It may be white, it may be black, it may have art on it, it might not……It's an ever changing open air gallery basically.

The artist Arofish was the first to paint this wall white (using the old trick of posing as a workman) and then come back later to add some art to it.

Since then it's had a succession of art and paint overs, including one cheeky reference by El Chivo to the repainting.

I wonder what it will look like when you visit?

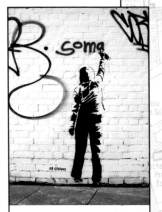

Soma' by El Chivo, June 2006, followed by 'paint it black…paint it white…' by El Chivo, Oct 2006 (Both painted over)

Next
Walk Up City Rd (A501).

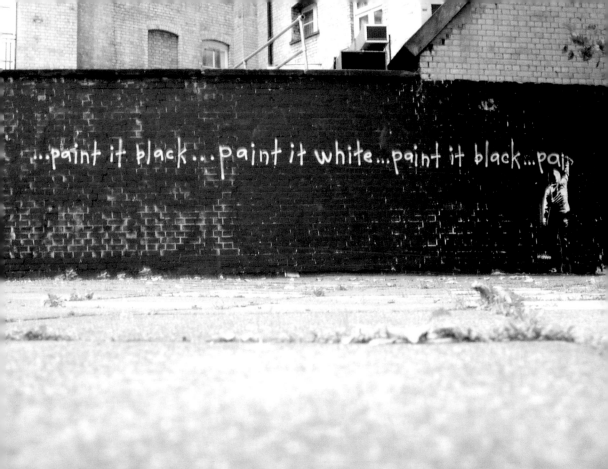

MICROPHONE RAT

Post Code - EC1V 9EH
Map / GPS reference - TQ 32551 82701

Location
Moorfields Eye Hospital, City Road (by Cayton St).

This is on an old disused entrance to Moorfields Eye Hospital and is a great example of a large microphone rat, although I like to think of it as a rat belting out 'My Way' on a karaoke machine or maybe toasting at a sweaty sound system clash in Kingston.

For half of 2006 it was covered up during renovations, but it managed to survive. Workers told me it wasn't due to be buffed, so I hope it will stay.

Status
Was released again in October 2006 and is visible again.

Next
Cross City Rd (A501), into Westland Place.

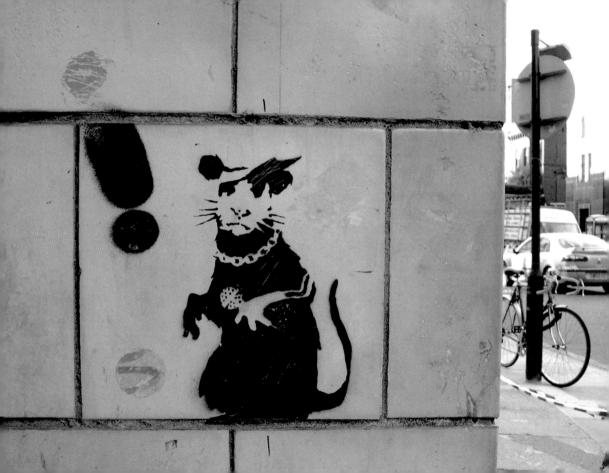

CUTTING RATS

Post Code - N1 7LP
Map / GPS reference - TQ 32551 82807

Location
Outside Fifteen Restaurant, Westland Place

Being an advocate for tree hugging pinko liberals...... Banksy did this stencil next to Jamie Oliver's 'social restaurant' Fifteen in oh so trendy Hoxton (he also did the same stencil on the gates to the Greenpeace office in London) as if some rats were breaking into it. Is there no end to this man's humour? ☺

There used to be a gangsta rat just around the corner but that has gone (see inset photo)

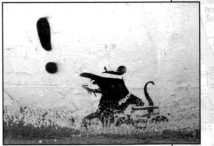

Status
Still there.

Next
Walk up Vestry St, until it joins East Rd.

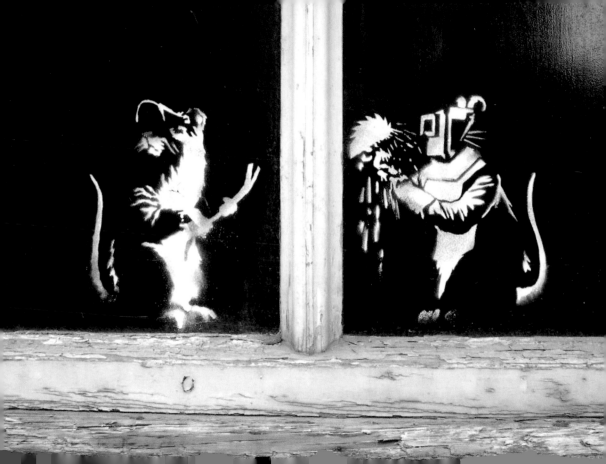

Post Code - N1 7LP
Map / GPS reference - TQ 32551 82807

Location
Slightly tucked away, on the corner of Vestry St and East Rd

Banksy's 'Smiley' Copper on a rather peeling wall, after having been amended
by an artist unknown to make it a rather unique 'blank faced' copper instead.
Also rather uniquely, a big Banksy tag covers the stomach area.

This exact graffiti is mentioned in Banksy's book 'Wall & Piece'

Status
Still there, although it is steadily peeling away, and the wall to the left has
been freshly painted, which is a bit ominous

Next
If you fancy a bit of a walk, continue up the New North Rd to S6 and S7.
Otherwise go straight to S8.

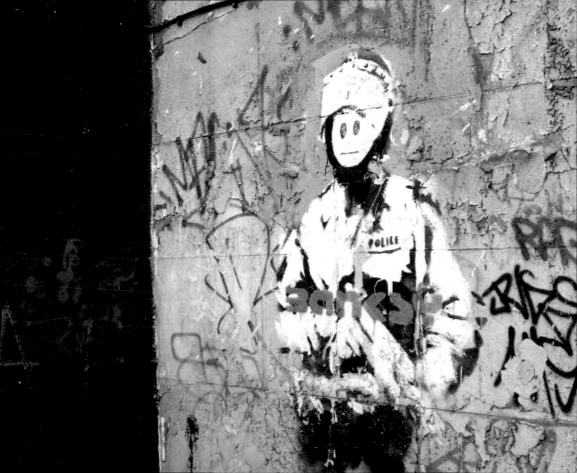

GIRL WITH BALLOON

Post Code - N1 6TA
Map / GPS reference - TQ 32696 83342

Location
On the side of some flats on the New North Rd (A1200),
close to Wimbourne St

Well worth the walk. The last remaining example of the
iconic Girl With Balloon.

Sometime around Spring 2006 the balloon was repainted,
by a person unknown.

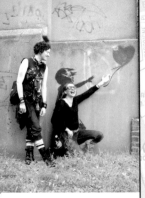

Erika & Nhatt at the
Girl With Balloon

Status
Still there.

Next
Continue up the new North Rd, and down Eagle Wharf Rd.

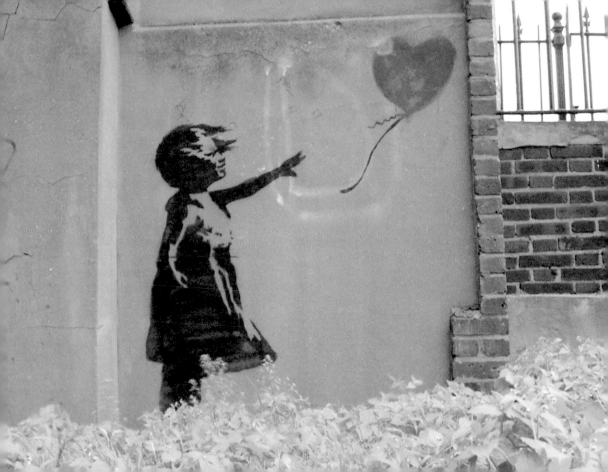

Post Code - N1 7QR
Map / GPS reference - TQ 32278 83371

Location
Under the foot bridge over the Grand Union Canal.
Sheperdess Walk / Eagle Wharf Rd

Best viewed from the bridge or the canal tow path.

A good example of how (I assume) Banksy re-uses stencils, as it seems the same as the one used for 'Tourist Information' just off the Hackney Rd (Ion Square - now sadly faded into obscurity)

Status
Still there.

Next
Retrace your steps, back towards East Rd.

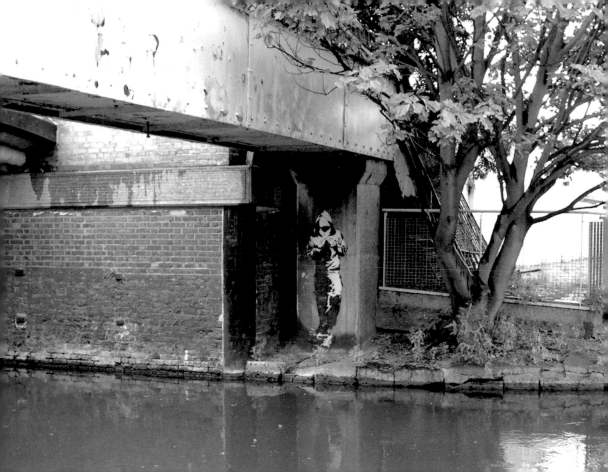

UMBRELLA RAT

Post Code - N1 6JB
Map / GPS reference - TQ 32877 83049

Location
On a lovely house, next to the newsagents on the corner of East Rd and New
North Rd

A great little Umbrella rat used to live in the corner of a large white section
of this house.

I think there was other graffiti there as well, before the wall was whitewashed,
but the Banksy was saved.

Six months later though the whole wall was painted over....

Status
Painted over.

Next
Continue down New North Rd, into Pitfield St.

58

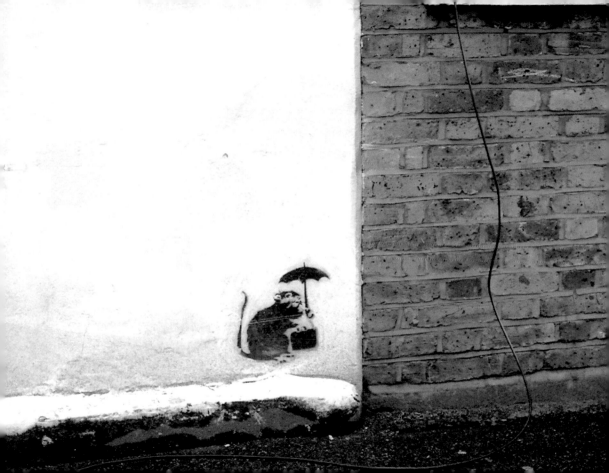

UMBRELLA RAT

Post Code - N1 6BU
Map / GPS reference - TQ 33014 82852

Location
On the metal newsagents box of City Supermarket, 57 Pitfield St
(near Haberdasher St).

A pretty awful specimen, with loads of runs, but it's a good example of how
these metal newsagent boxes are a great target for graffiti artists as they are
left out all night for secure milk and newspaper deliveries.

Status
Buffed (circa December 2006).

Next
Continue down Pitfield St.

BLT TIP
I don't eat animal products so I
can't judge the kebabs for you,
but the 'Best Kebab & Café' at
the bottom of Pitfield St does a
lovely falafel meal, and the cof-
fee and the service is great too.

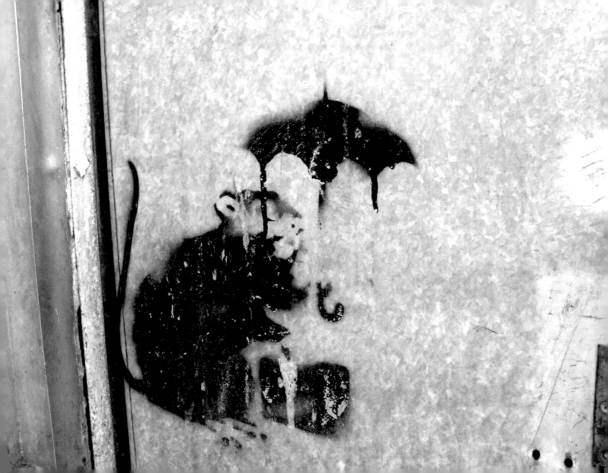

Post Code - EC2A 3JD
Map / GPS reference - TQ 32978 82519

Location
Above 'Wa Do Chinese Fast Food' shop on the corner of Old Street &
Tabernacle St.

This is now rather ironically obscured by the massive advertising hoardings
above, and the shop sign below.

There is a great photo of this in the snow in Banksy's books, when it used to
be Franco's Fish & Chips shop.

Status
Still there, but very obscured.

Next
Cross over half of Old Street by the Foundry.

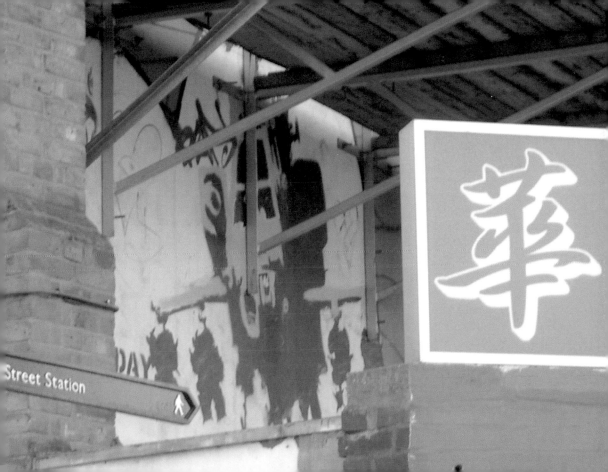

LOOK DOWN TO THE PULP FICTION SITE

Post Code - EC1V 9PB
Map / GPS reference - TQ 32834 82543

Location
Above a row of shops on Old St, near Vine St.
One of the most famous sites in London, but also very hard to photograph and view. Staying further away, often gives you a better view of it.

For several years it had Banksy's famous Pulp Fiction piece on it. In May 2006 Shepard Fairey put a massive Obey poster up, and Faile flanked it on both sides with their snarling dog wheat pastes. 'Banksy was ere' was also crudely added on top in a pink paint that looked suspiciously the same shade that both faile and Banksy had recently used around town. Then in July a new version of Pulp Fiction went up, followed in September with a complete paste over, and then a crude 'Nothing Lasts Forever'.
As they say, great art is all in the composition…..

Status
it's likely to change by the time I've even finished this sentence…..

Next Turn into Rivington St.

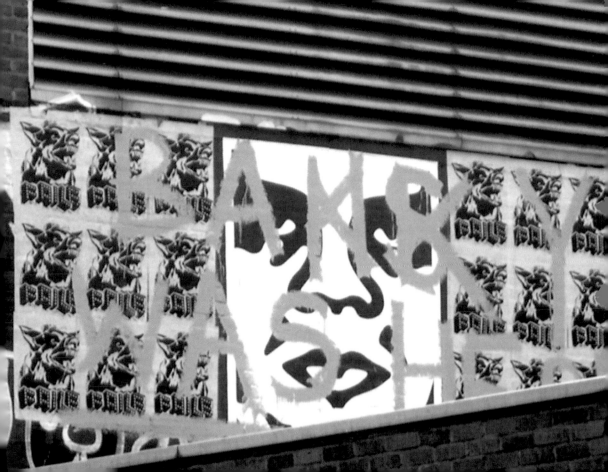

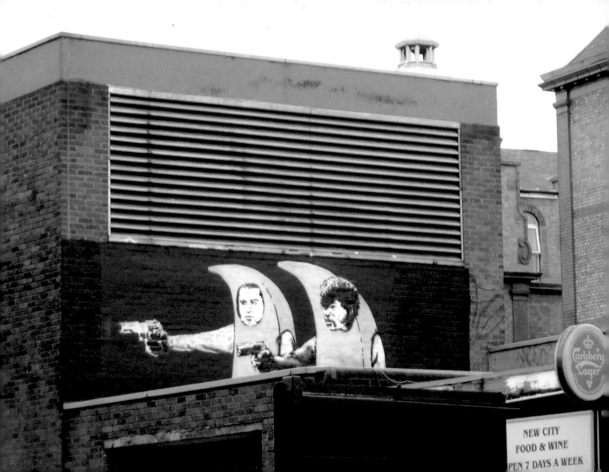

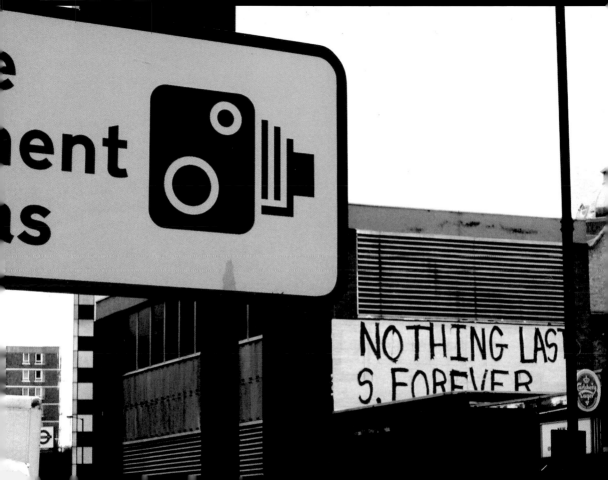

TV OUT OF THE WINDOW & GIANT RAT

Post Code - EC2A 3DT
Map / GPS reference - TQ 33059 82549

Location
In a private car park on the corner of Rivington St and
Old St / Great Eastern St.

Another great site, which includes Banksy's TV out of the Window, and an
enormous rat with a knife and fork (similar size and shape to the cat done in
Liverpool for the 2004 Art Biennial).

The private car park seems to operate irregular opening hours, but it's best to
see the art when the gates are open. Ask politely and they'll probably let you
in to see them up close.

Status
Both still there.

Next
Cross over Great Eastern St.

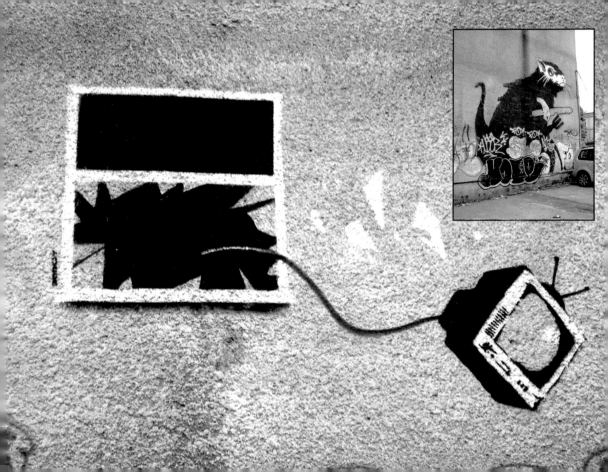

GRIN REAPER

Post Code - EC2A 4NY
Map / GPS reference - TQ 33003 82467

Location
On the side of a bar called 'Yard' on the corner of Paul St and Tabernacle St.

A very faded Grin Reaper. Hardly worth mentioning, but a good example of something that fades away, or is buffed to within an inch of its life....

Status
Very faded.

Next
Continue down Paul St, past the large metal sculpture on Leonard St that used to be a favourite spot for graffitists, stickerists and bill posters, until it was completely stripped, cleaned and painted in some anti-graffiti coating in Sept 2006. In October, Blek Le Rat was the first to get anything to stick on it, but it only lasted a few days...

S13

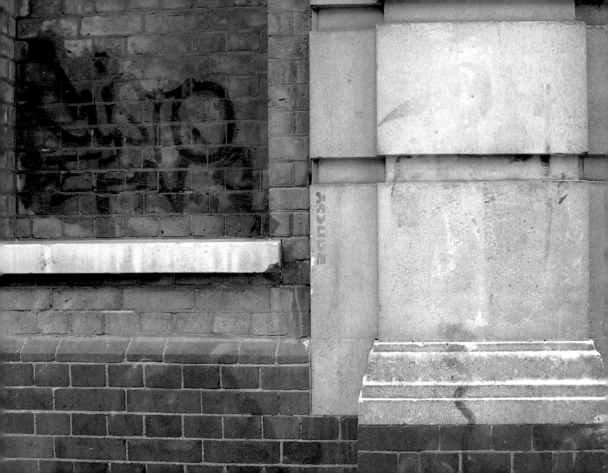

GRIN REAPER

Post Code - EC2A 4RT
Map / GPS reference - TQ 33030 82209

Location
On Scrutton St, near Clifton St.

A stunning yellow Grin Reaper on a blue wall where the old Pictures On Walls office used to be.

Status
Still there.

Next
Continue down Scrutton St.

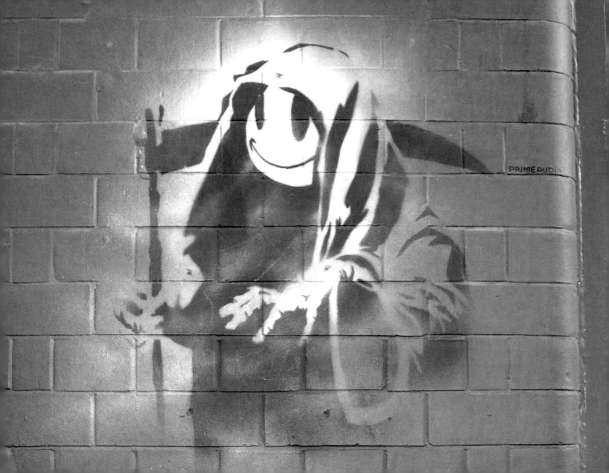

HAPPY CHOPPERS

Post Code - EC2A 4XB
Map / GPS reference - TQ 33113 82180

Location
On Holywell Row.

Tucked away behind a blind corner. Very faded but the only approachable Happy Choppers that are left.

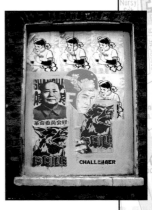

There are usually some faile paste ups on the building opposite (see the inset photo - this is a sort of unofficial faile history site that they post on every time they come over to London)

Status
Poorly painted over in December 2006 (the top of one helicopter is still visible!). The faile section opposite was also stripped bare at the same time.

Next
Go back to Scrutton St and continue along.

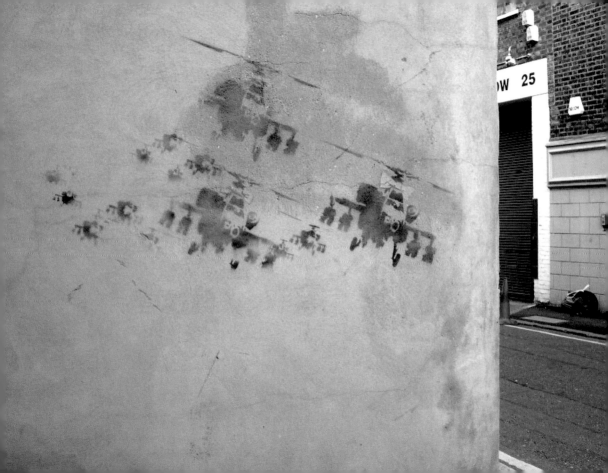

WAITER RATS

Post Code - EC2A 3PT
Map / GPS reference - TQ 33259 82286

Location
On the corner of Curtain Rd & Christina St, by Pizza Express

I first photographed this in January 2006 and by the time
I went back a week or so later it had pretty much gone
(I often revisit sites - and also I had stupidly lost all my
digital photos from the January visit!).

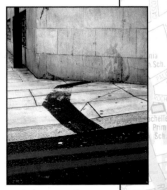

Status
The rats are barely noticeable, but the red 'carpet' is still
quite visible on the pavement. See inset photo.

Next
Head up Curtain Rd.

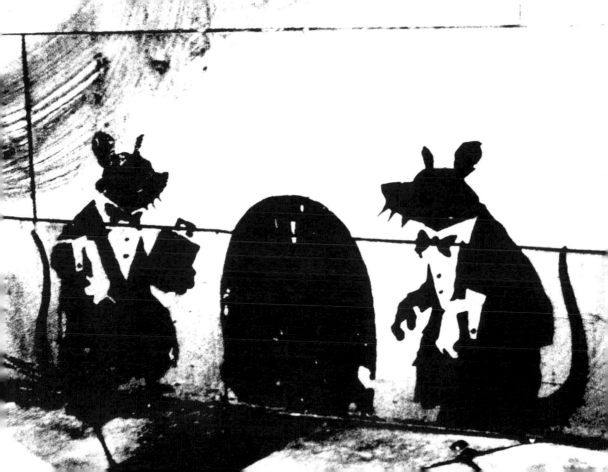

BLT TIP

Watch out in this area for the new style Eine alphabet (C & F) on roadside boxes on Curtain Rd, an old El Chivo off New Yard Inn, and a large Space Invader in the distance, on the rail bridge.

It's always worth wandering around the New Yard Inn area, especially the blind spots around the side & back of 'The Old Blue Last' pub, as they are often covered with art.

Over the years a Girl With Balloon and a pissing soldier have been there, but they went quite a while ago.

The photo shows us in the New Yard Inn area, whilst on a tour of Shoreditch.

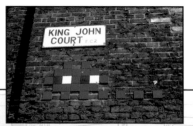
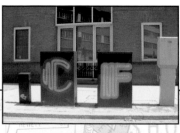

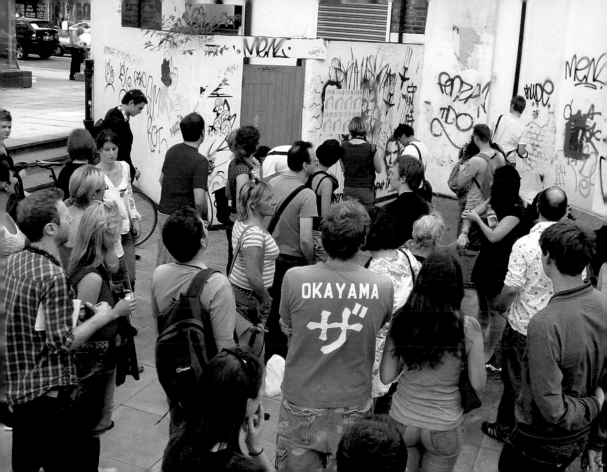

DESIGNATED PICNIC AREAS

Post Code - EC2A 3AH
Map / GPS reference - TQ 33294 82478

Location
1) On the small steps of a derelict building on Curtain Rd
   (near Curtain Place)
2) On the Curtain Rd end of a skanky alley
   (Dereham Place)

Two faded but enigmatic 'Designated Picnic Areas'.
The one on the steps is one of my favourites anywhere.
The entrance it's on is usually plastered with old
posters and litter, and has looked liked that for ages.

Status
(1) faded, but visible (2) Buffed circa December 2006

Next
Cross the road towards 'The Elbow Room'.

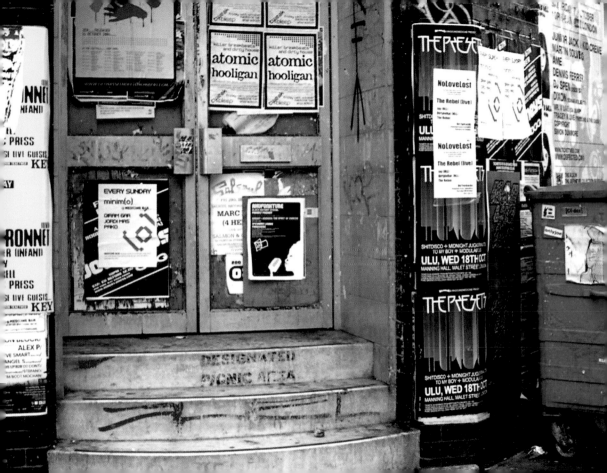

SNORTING COPPER
& WHITE LINE

Post Code - EC2A 3BS
Map / GPS reference - TQ 33249 82500

Location
The Snorting Copper was just off Curtain Rd (by 'The Elbow Room' Pool Lounge & Bar). The white line goes along the alley (Mills Court) and into a drain on Charlotte Rd.

One day in May 2006 the Council came along and badly jet washed this (see inset photo). Ironically it then looked far worse! At least this art was making an attempt to brighten up the streets and get our brains thinking.

A version still exists at Waterloo Station (see R6)

Status
Buffed in May 2006, but with a touch of mimicry of the Waterloo one, there is now a (dodgy looking) Space Invader above it.

BLT TIP
This alley (Mills Court) often has good graffiti in it. A good El Chivo may still be there when you visit.

Next
Walk up Charlotte Rd.

S18

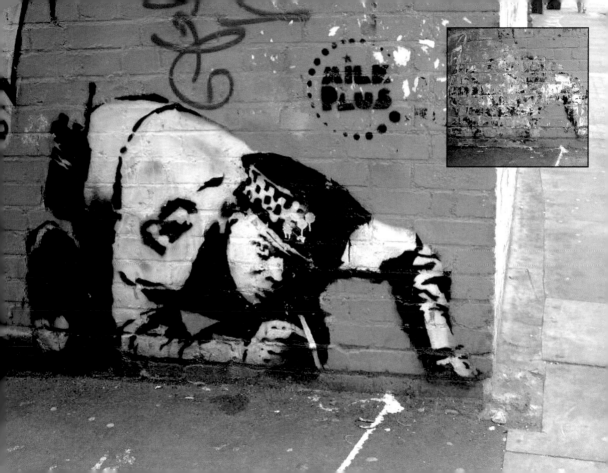

THE MAID

Post Code - EC2A 3PT
Map / GPS reference - TQ 33259 82286

Location
Was on the side of the White Cube Gallery (Rufus St side)

On the side of Jay Joplin's White Cube gallery in Hoxton Square for about 6 weeks in mid 2006 before they probably decided it was too much competition for their own exhibits and painted over it.

Status
Painted Over (still vaguely traceable if you look hard).

Next
Walk along Hoxton Square, back to Old St.

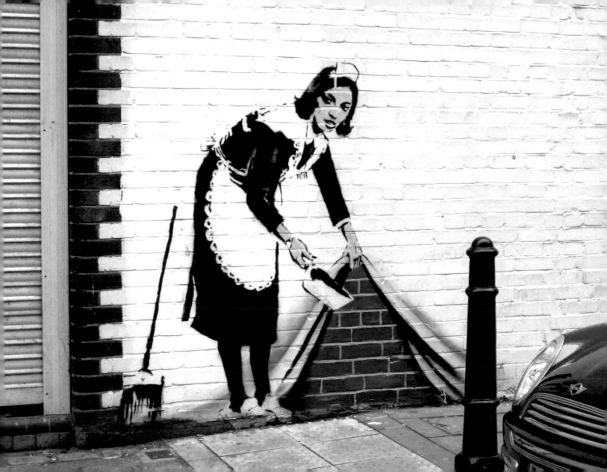

ABANDON HOPE
OLD ST BRIDGE

Post Code - EC1V 9LP
Map / GPS reference - TQ 33371 82674

Location
Train Bridge across Old St (near Shoreditch High St).

Another Banksy icon. And one of the few times Banksy used pasted up posters. Over several years Banksy regularly added images and messages to this bridge.

The final message was 'Abandon Hope' in Spring 2006, which only lasted a week or so....

Status
Bits of the Smiley Soldiers were still visible for a while, until the bridge was completely stripped and repainted in Sept 2006. But I bet Banksy won't be able to resist targeting it again one day!

Next
Turn up Kingsland Rd and walk up to Cremer St.

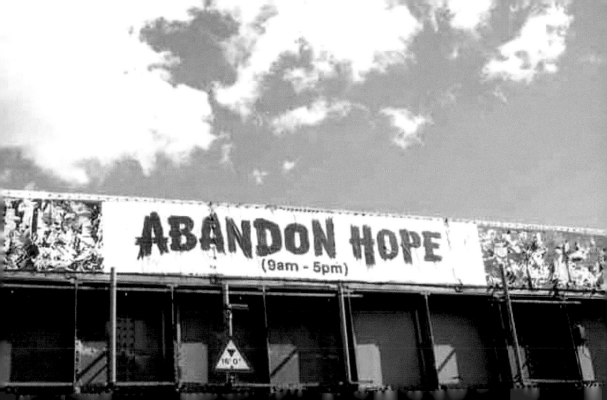

CUTTING RAT

Post Code - E2 8EA
Map / GPS reference - TQ 33573 83118

Location
On metal doors to one of the 'underneath the arches' workshops on Geffrye St.

Only one cutting rat this time, but because it's cutting into the padlock, it gives it a marvellous contextual power.

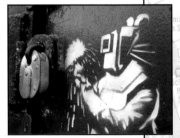

Status
Still there. Although I fear the whole area may get redeveloped soon due to the tube line extension.

Next
Walk along Cremer St, & cross the Hackney Rd.

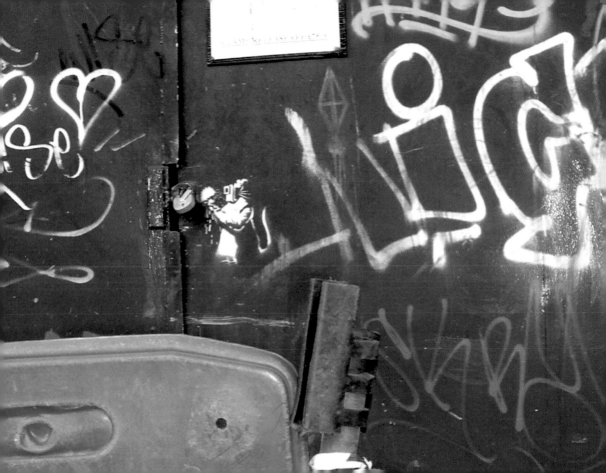

PARACHUTE RAT

Post Code - E2 7RA
Map / GPS reference - TQ 33712 82975

Location
Diss St. This was the best, and most photogenic parachute rat around until it fell foul of the Council clean up campaign.

Status
Buffed (circa December 2006).

Next
Return to the Hackney Rd, and turn right, heading away from Shoreditch.

ALTERNATIVELY - Miss out S23 by returning to the Hackney Rd, and heading down it, back towards Shoreditch.

Several Eine'd shop shutters (and Eine's illusion piece) exist on Hackney Rd, and the Gorsuch Place area is often awash with art.

S22

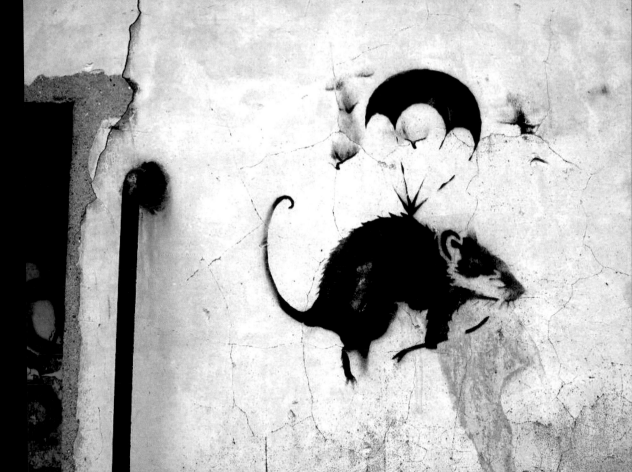

KEEP IT REAL

Post Code - E2 7QB
Map / GPS reference - TQ 33927 82885

Location
Towards the bottom of Ravenscroft St, close to Columbia Rd.

There is only one rule in life. Yes, really.... just one. You can never have enough monkeys.

That's it. Sorry if I have now spoiled the meaning of life for you, but you had to know sooner or later. Oh, and whilst I'm making peoples lives better I'll let you into a secret.....The tooth fairies don't really leave you money in return for your teeth; it's your parents.

Never the greatest graffiti (it was very small and hence the detail was poor) but for a long time it was the only surviving example around

Status
Buffed (circa December 2006).

S25

Next
Walk down Columbia Rd, onto the Hackney Rd and into Shoreditch High St.

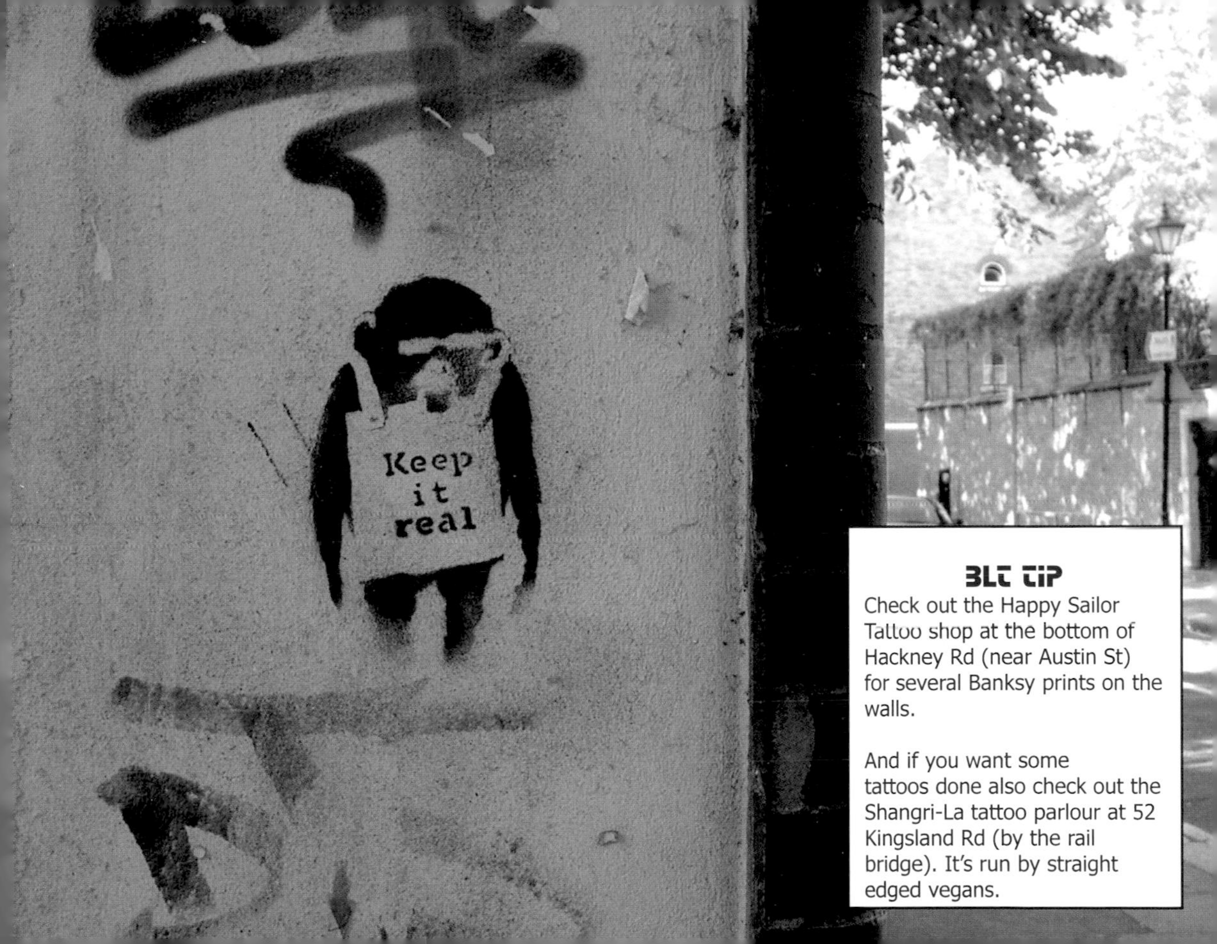

Keep
it
real

BLT TiP

Check out the Happy Sailor
Tattoo shop at the bottom of
Hackney Rd (near Austin St)
for several Banksy prints on the
walls.

And if you want some
tattoos done also check out the
Shangri-La tattoo parlour at 52
Kingsland Rd (by the rail
bridge). It's run by straight
edged vegans.

Boy & paint brush - Post Code - EC2A 3AY
Map / GPS reference - TQ 33379 82551

Cargo - Post Code - EC2A 3AZ
Map / GPS reference - TQ 33374 82586

Designated Picnic Area - Post Code - EC2A 3BE
Map / GPS reference - TQ 33363 82594

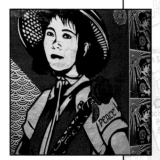

Location
Rivington St, near Shoreditch High St (A10).

Status
1 = Buffed.
2 & 3 = still there.

Next
Return to Shoreditch High St, and head south.

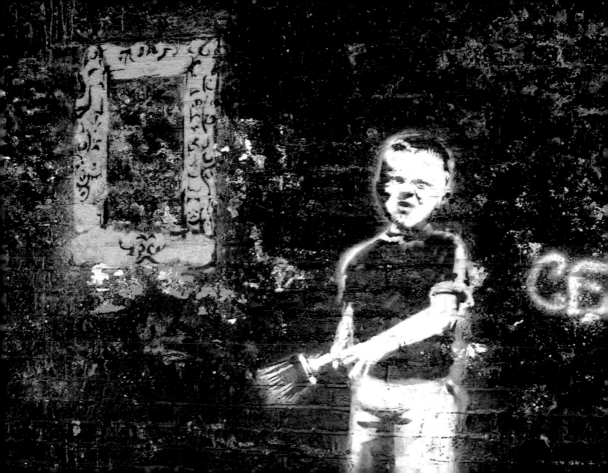

THE 'CARGO' AREA

Cargo is often referred to as a super club as it's so damn cool. It has pretty much supported Banksy from the start and two of his works still remain in the back courtyard, which seems to be great respect as many of the other walls in the courtyard are rotated with new art.

The Guard and Poodle (and designated graffiti area) dominate the first wall. The courtyard is often open - for free - when the club isn't charging for entrance to the main club, although since they added wooden decking and loads of greenery in mid 2006 it is harder to see and photograph.

A few walls away (past some great Shepard Fairey paste-ups, see inset photo) Banksy's HMV image remains, surrounded by other graffiti from Stylo of the VOP crew - check out www.vopstars.com

Just outside the club, a slightly forlorn 'kid with paint brush' lurked under the railway bridge until badly buffed in November 2006. Of the four times this image was used in London, this one seems to be the least finished, or in a well chosen environment. I wonder if it was a job half finished..?

Finally there is a 'Designated Picnic Area' and arrow in an alley (Standard Place) just a short distance from Cargo. The black & silver bubble graf around it actually enhances it in my opinion.

BY ORDER
NATIONAL HIGHWAYS AGENCY

THIS WALL IS A DESIGNATED
GRAFFITI AREA

PLEASE TAKE YOUR LITTER HOME
EC. REF. URBA 23/366

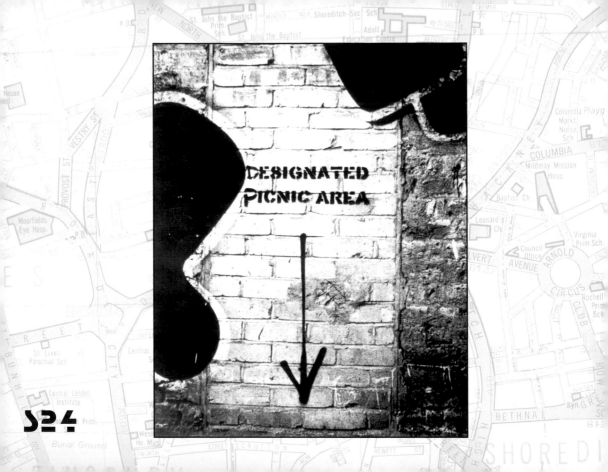

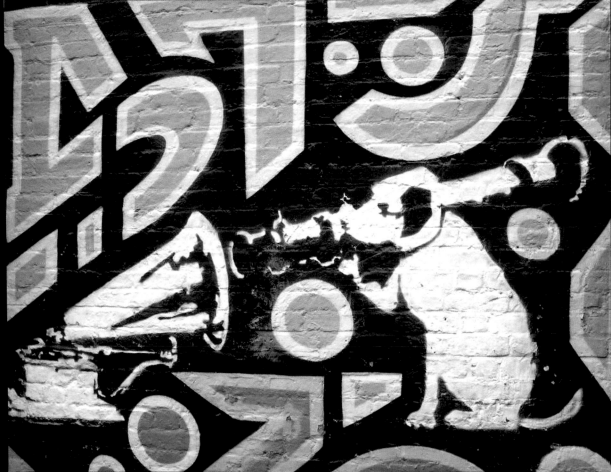

BANKSY TAG

Post Code - E2 7HX
Map / GPS reference - TQ 33741 82409

Location
On the Turville St side of 'Anisha Cash & Carry',
Redchurch St.

Only the Banksy tag survives (inside the utilities box)
but above it a sawing rat used to exist.

See the Banksy books (e.g. Existencilism) to see what
it looked like before.

Status
The tag is still there.

Next
Walk slightly back, then down Club Row and across
the Bethnal Green Rd (A1209).

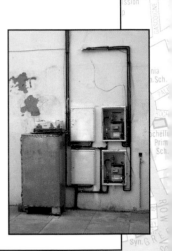

S25

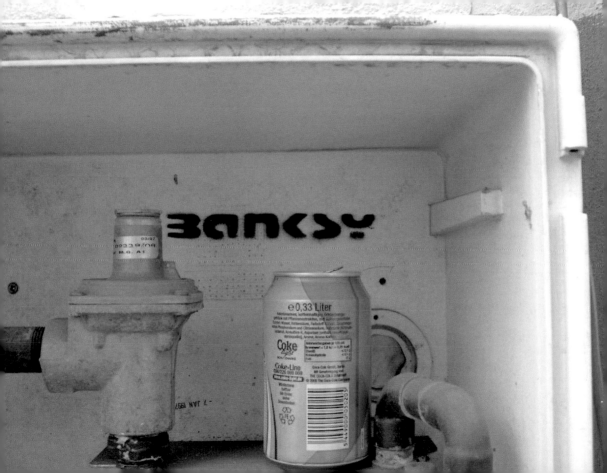

PARACHUTE RAT

Post Code - E1 6HT
Map / GPS reference - TQ 33733 82291

Location
On the side of an abandoned building on Sclater St, near the Bethnal Green Rd (A1209).

A faded Parachute Rat just survives, sometimes hidden by the overgrowth. Note a great illusion style 'Cept' on the shutters to the abandoned building.

There is also an ever changing gallery of street art along the walls of Sclater St, usually including more from Cept.

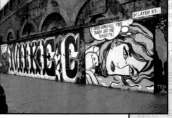

Status
Still there.

Next
Continue along Sclater St, turn right into Brick Lane, then first left into Grimsby St.

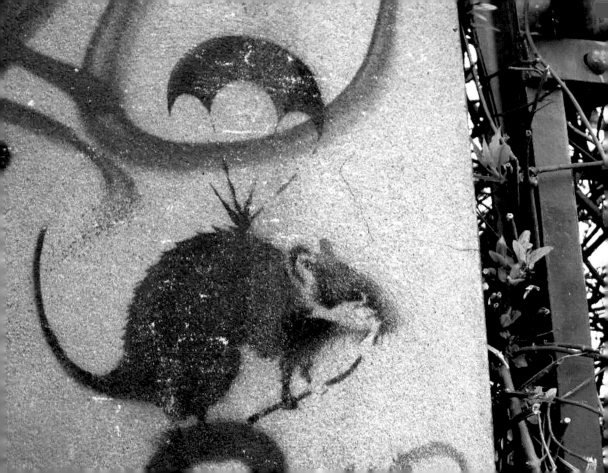

PARACHUTE RAT & BANKSY TAG

Post Code - E2 6ES
Map / GPS reference - TQ 33930 82233

Location
A good Parachute Rat used to exist amidst the gallery of street art and market shops along Grimsby St. Tentacles were later added to it by a person unknown, and now it has almost disappeared (see inset photo).

Don't be fooled by the small Banksy tag on the wall further down the street. The large alien / baby figures near by are NOT by Banksy. They are by Mr.Yu, a Japanese artist. The tag relates to a Banksy piece that used to be there; I still have never managed to find out exactly what was there!

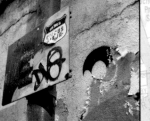

Status
The rat has pretty much gone, but the tag is still there, and it's a lovely vibrant street in general. It may all be under threat from the tube line extension though!

Next
Return to Brick Lane, towards the old Truman Brewery.

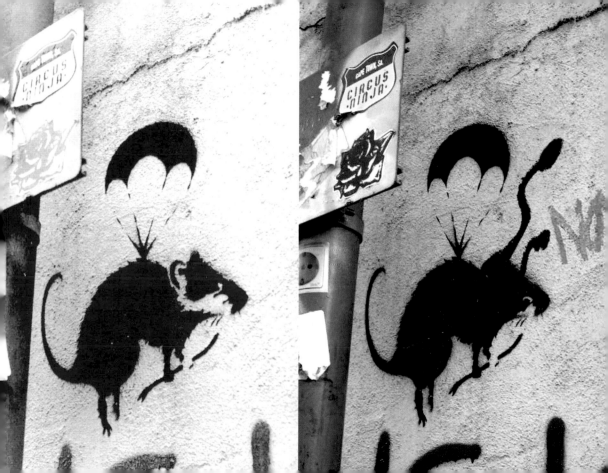

Post Code - E2 6ES
Map / GPS reference - TQ 33911 82220

Location
Brick Lane, by the old Shoreditch tube station (now closed).

This exact graffiti is shown in the Wall & Piece book. Seeing this in the flesh is a great sight (with Eine's version opposite - bloody graffiti artists!). Be careful of the achingly stupid looking Shoreditch fashion victims and the Sunday street sellers.

Status
Still there, although showing signs of age, and can become a little obscured by the trees in the summer.

Next
Continue down Brick Lane.

BLT TIP
There are several fading Arofish stencils nearby, and the wall down to the old tube station is usually worth checking out.

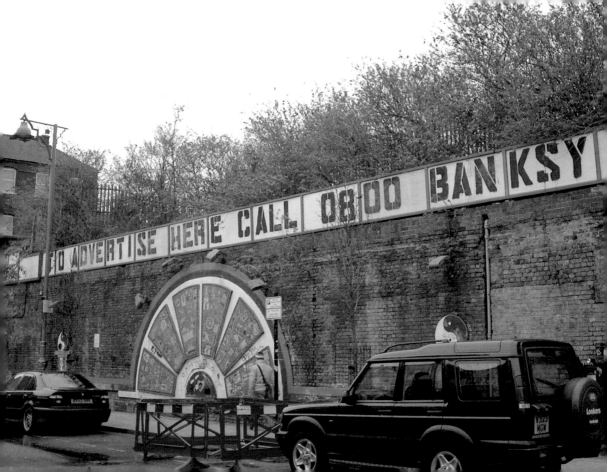

Post Code - E1 5HD
Map / GPS reference - TQ 33893 82003

Location
Brick Lane, opposite the main entrance to the old Truman Brewery.

Banksy hit several lampposts and CCTV poles around London, putting up plastic crows with pirate flags, fags, and pulling at wires.

A Banksy tag exists on this pole, so I assume this was one of those sites at some point in the past?

Status
Tag still there

Next
Continue just a few metres down Brick Lane, to the corner with Woodseer St.

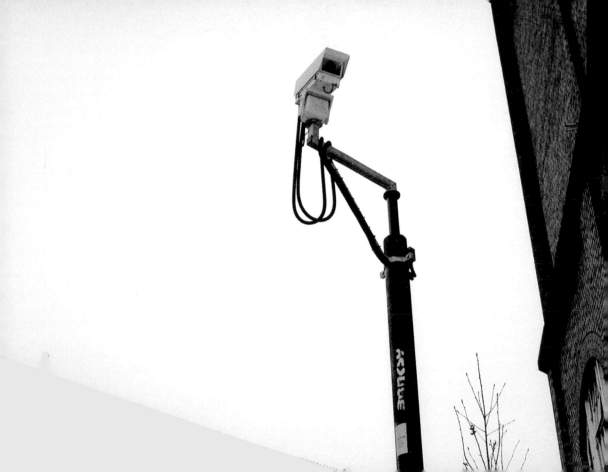

Post Code - E1 5HD
Map / GPS reference - TQ 33895 81983

Location
Brick Lane, on the corner with Woodseer St.

Very faded, but it's the only example I know of in London.

Status
Rather faded and often attacked by the remnants of fly posters.

Next
Return up Brick Lane a few metres, and go into the old Truman Brewery area.

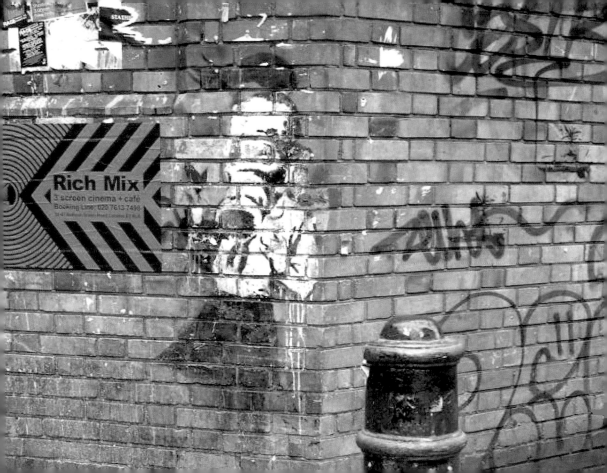

Rich Mix

3 screen cinema + café

Booking Line: 020 7613 7498

35-47 Bethnal Green Road, London, E1 6LA

PiNK CAR

Post Code - E1 5HD
Map / GPS reference - TQ 33893 82003

Location
On top of an old shipping container, in the main concourse area of the old Truman Brewery area.

I've never quite found out the reason for this, but an old car has been given the Banksy treatment. A Banksy tag exists on the far right of the container. Many photographers make sure they get 'the Gherkin' in the background to their photo of this. I prefer to get the skanky derelict old graffiti / drugs / alchy / prossie den in the background (it's on Grey Eagle St, but last time I looked it had been locked up!) Pieces by Space Invader, Dscreet, Obey, D*face and Faile can often also be seen in this whole area.

Status
Still there. But in November 2006 it was covered with a horrible seethrough box! At least D*face's car (see inset photo) now gives it some company.

The End
Carry on wandering around the area if you want (there is so much to see!). Or if you need a tube station, continue down Brick Lane to Aldgate East tube station, or through the side streets to Liverpool St station. Alternatively, a new tube station in Shoreditch may be open by the time you read this book.

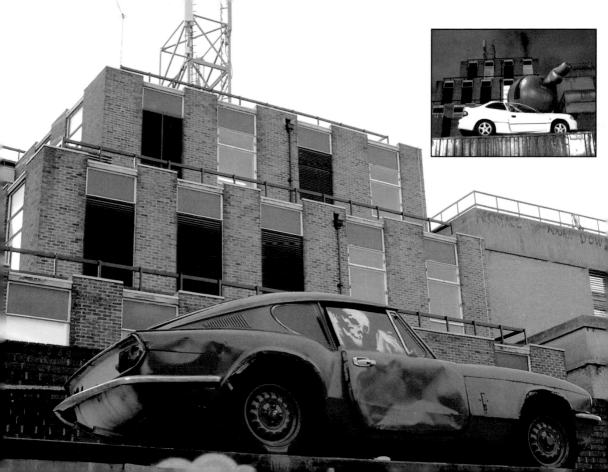

FARRINGDON

&

CLERKENWELL

TOUR

INTRODUCTION

This tour goes around the Barbican / Smithfields area, then heads up to Clerkenwell, Hatton Garden, and finally Farringdon Rd and Exmouth Market, ending up by the enormous Mount Pleasant sorting office.

Assuming they are still there by the time the reader may visit, the tour includes loads of excellent quality rats (especially in the Barbican area that I call 'rat city'), the Cash Machine & Girl, and Thugs for Life (or 'old skool' as some know it now). Plus two enormous Blek Le Rat's and some Obey (Shepard Fairey) and D*face paste-ups.

This mini-tour is not a very long way, and as it's all relatively flat and doesn't involve any nonavoidable steps I would have thought that it could be done by someone using a wheelchair or a baby buggy.

You won't need a tube / bus / whatever ticket for this... It's just a bit of walking. When I did it as a tour it took us just over 1½ hours.

STArT

The closest tube stations from the first location are Moorgate (Northern, Circle, Metropolitan, and Hammersmith & City tube lines, plus selected rail services), Barbican (Circle, Metropolitan, and Hammersmith & City tube lines), and Liverpool St (Central, Circle, Metropolitan, and Hammersmith & City lines, plus many National rail services).

It's also not that far from Old Street station as well. If you don't have a map the best place to start might be Barbican tube, although it will (rather annoyingly) involve returning to the station after the first location. When you come out of Barbican tube follow the yellow signs and yellow line that are on the pavement (marked 'Barbican Centre'). This will take you through the covered underpass (Beech St).

As you come out of the underpass carry on (slight kink in the road to the right) for about another 100 metres and the Banksy placard rat ('London Doesn't Work') is straight in front of you, on a white wall outside 39/40 Chiswell St (just before the 'St Paul's Tavern', which is on the other side of the road).

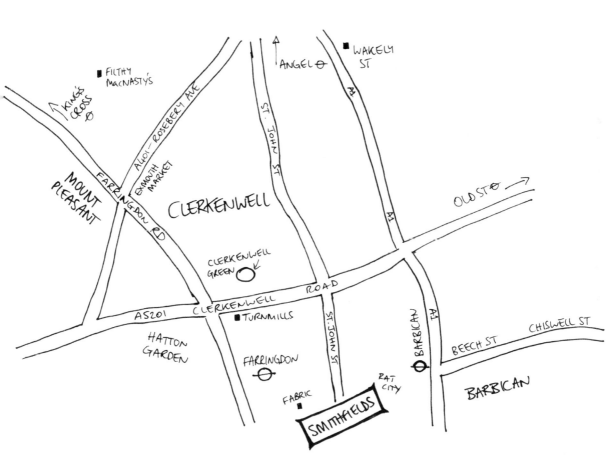

PLACARD RAT
'LONDON DOESN'T WORK'

Post Code - EC1Y 4SB
Map / GPS reference - TQ 32497 81970

Location
Chiswell St, near Lamb's Passage.

This is a brilliant example of Banksy's placard rat, this time announcing that 'London Doesn't Work'. This is one of the most popular black & white photos that I sell. In a stroke of genius I took my photo of it with a London taxi going past (surely one of the iconic images of London - not that I'm saying taxi drivers are what makes London not work - Terry 'The Knuckles' Wilson won't let me say that and nor would my dear departed Dad!).

Unfortunately it was a silver taxi and not the black version! Tough. Take your own photo if you prefer, smart arse. ☺

Status
Still there.

Next
Walk towards barbican tube, through the Beech St underpass.
Cross Aldersgate by Barbican tube station, and continue into Long Lane.

F1

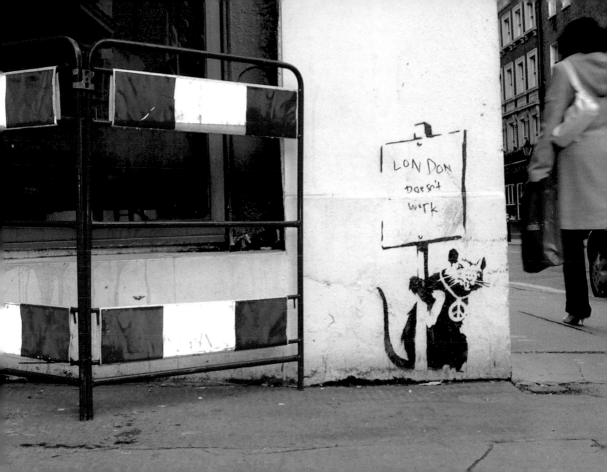

FADED PLACARD RAT

Post Code - EC1A 9HF
Map / GPS reference - TQ 32065 81844

Location
On Long Lane, just around the corner from Barbican tube station.

A very faded Placard Rat. Hardly worth mentioning, but a good example of how this one (on the main road) has been buffed to within an inch of its life, whereas the gaggle of rats (or litter, or gang, or parliament, or whatever it is...) around the corner are treated as preserved works of art!

Status
Hard to see, even if you know where it is!

Next
Continue along Long Lane a short distance, and into Hayne St.

F2

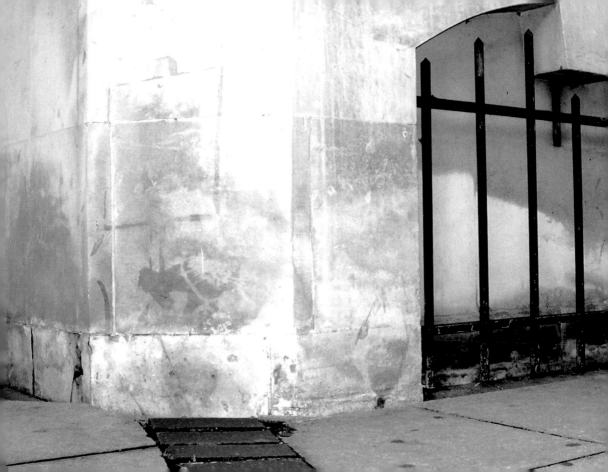

THE RAT PACK

Post Code - EC1A 9HG
Map / GPS reference - TQ 31941 81847

Location
All within 20 metres of each other, on Hayne St & Charterhouse Square.

Banksy obviously had a bit of mentalist moment in the Barbican area one night. Within 20 metres there are 4 different stencils adorning the walls. B, c & d (see below) are all on the same building and when it got repainted they actually painted around the Banksy pieces, thus preserving them! Respect.

Status
All are still there, but 3 have been painted around, which sort of spoils it a bit. Could be worse though, they could be gone!

Next
Take the detour to F7, or continue along Charterhouse Square / Street towards F4.

F3

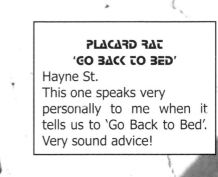

PLACARD RAT
'GO BACK TO BED'
Hayne St.
This one speaks very personally to me when it tells us to 'Go Back to Bed'. Very sound advice!

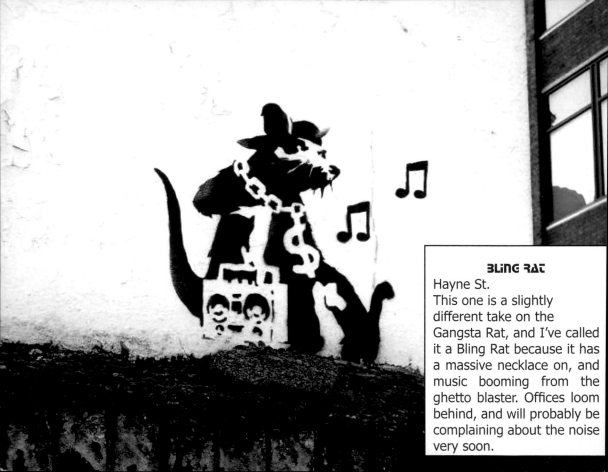

BLING RAT
Hayne St.
This one is a slightly different take on the Gangsta Rat, and I've called it a Bling Rat because it has a massive necklace on, and music booming from the ghetto blaster. Offices loom behind, and will probably be complaining about the noise very soon.

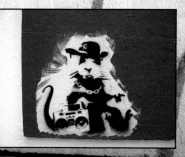

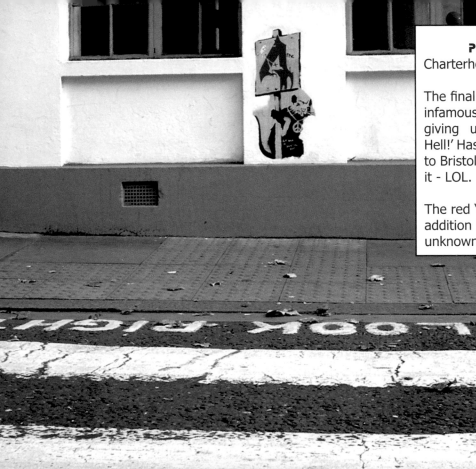

PLACARD RAT
Charterhouse Square.

The final one of the infamous 'Barbican Four', giving us a 'Welcome to Hell!' Has since had 'Go back to Bristol boy' scrawled onto it - LOL.

The red '4' is also an addition by a person unknown...

GO BACK
TO
BRISTOL
BOY

BLT TIP
To see some other street art in
the area follow F4 & F5. If you
couldn't give a toss, go straight
to F7 for another Banksy.

FAILE STENCILS

Post Code - EC1A 9HL
Map / GPS reference - TQ 31943 81802

Location
On Lindsey St, opposite the East side of Smithfields market.

I spotted these early in June 2006, but they might have also been part of the Faile blitz in late May 2006 when the Faile peeps plastered Shoreditch with various examples of their name, and snarling dog wheatpastes.

Two fantastically detailed stencils ('Smoking' & 'Monster') are on the wall of an old 'Men's Lavatory' next to Smithfields market.

Status
A very bad attempt was made to buff it in early 2007.

Next
Join Long Lane again and continue along, as it becomes West Smithfield.

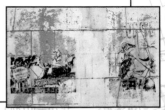

F4

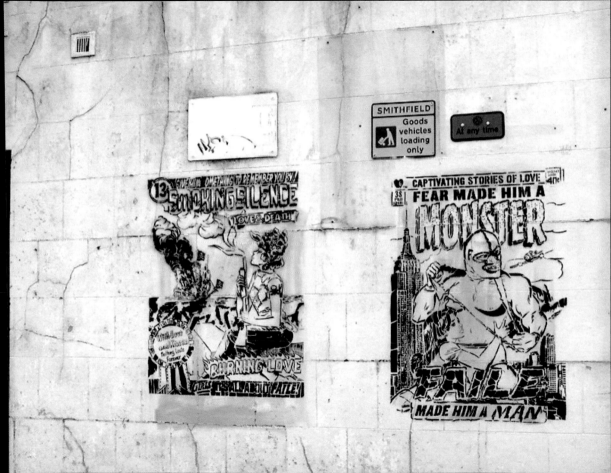

D*FACE - SKELETON QUEEN

Post Code - EC1A 9LY
Map / GPS reference - TQ 31594 81597

Location
On West Smithfield, close to Farringdon St (A201).

D*face is another great street and gallery artist. He celebrated the Queen's 80th birthday in 2006 by releasing a print and putting up these pastes in a few places in London, showing the Queen just in her bones. It's called 'Canis Servo Regina' which knowing D's obsessions probably means something like his previous print, 'Dog Save the Queen'.
I deliberately left the surroundings in the photo as that is partly what drew me to photograph the paste up in the first place. Smithfield's is a rather run down part of our heritage... bit like the Queen really....

Status
Pasted over with fly posters circa December 2006.

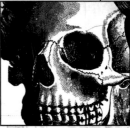

Next
Walk through / under the market, out onto Charterhouse St.

F5

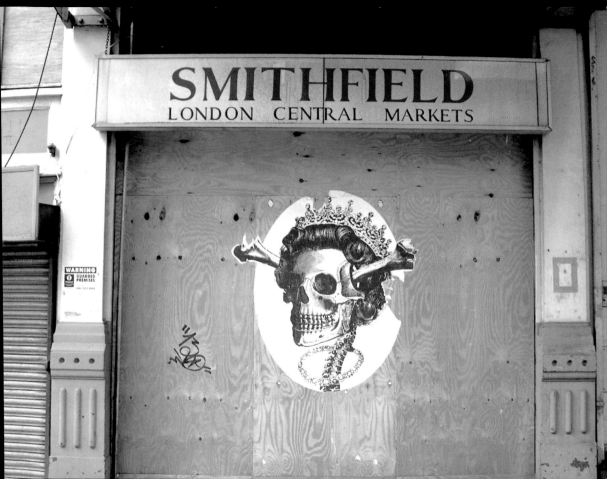

BOMB HUGGER

Map / GPS reference - TQ 31709 81783

Location
Inside 'Fabric' club, 77a Charterhouse St, EC1M 3HN.

For all you drum n bass heads out there, a night out at Fabric will not only make your jinglies jangle, but you can also check out a Banksy Bomb Hugger sprayed straight onto the wall, by the toilets.

They even put a frame around it…

Status
Still there.

Next
Continue along Charterhouse St, to St. John's St.

BLT TiP

On your way up St. John's St (between F7 & F8) check out the rear (i.e. facing up St.John's St) of a large traffic sign towards the junction with Clerkenwell Rd. Last time I looked it had large, and fresh, Obey and D*face posters on it.

Then check out two from Blek Le Rat, inside shops on the right hand side of St.John's St, approx opposite Aylesbury St.

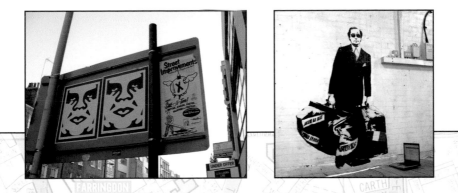

GANGSTA RAT

Post Code - EC1M 4BL
Map / GPS reference - TQ 31772 81903

Location
Floor level, near some railings on Peter's Lane (just off St. John's St).

Yeah yet another rat, but another good quality one and a very ironic addition to it. Someone has written 'not a banksy' on it, when in fact it looks like one of the clearest Banksy's I've ever seen. Sure, they can be faked (and there are some questionable ones out there), but I doubt this one is….

Status
Still there, but repetitious images of a woman's face were added to the right of it in early 2007.

Next
Continue up St. John's St.

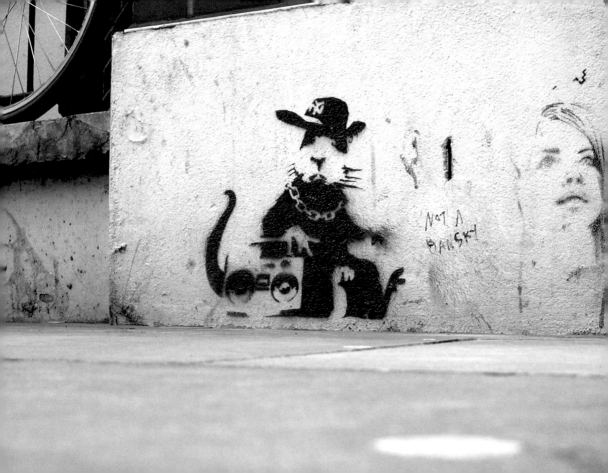

REFUSE STORE HANGING RAT

Post Code - EC1V 4JY
Map / GPS reference - TQ 31688 82363

Location
Bottom end of Agdon St (just off St. John's St / Compton St).

I love the placement of this likkle rat, hanging off a door marked 'Refuse Store'. The metal door gives a photo a grey tone, but if you play around with the image you can also get it into a nice contrasty black & white image.

Status
Still there.

Next
Return a short distance down St. John's St, and walk along Aylesbury St towards Clerkenwell Green

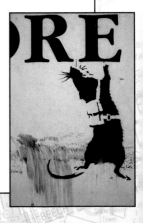

F8

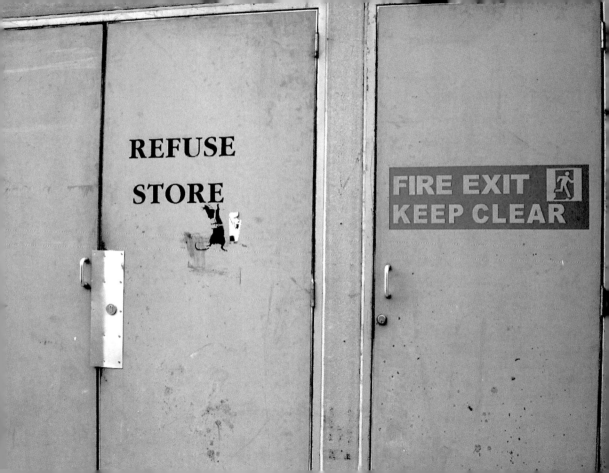

BLT TIP

If you are energetic you could continue up St. John's St, and then across Rawstorne St to see the Banksy vs Faile pieces on Wakely St (A501). Not only another great example of Banksy's 'kid' stencil, which he used at least four times in London around May 2006 (this time he is painting a heart on the wall), but also a great Faile stencil ('Fate').

If you are thirsty you might like to stop off at Filthy MacNasty's, a well known pub, at 68 Amwell Street, EC1. It's covered with music memorabilia, including some of favourite son Pete Doherty, whilst with The Libertines, and plays an eclectic mix of music. Lenin reputedly drank here in 1905. He's probably not been back for a while though.
www.filthymacnastys.com

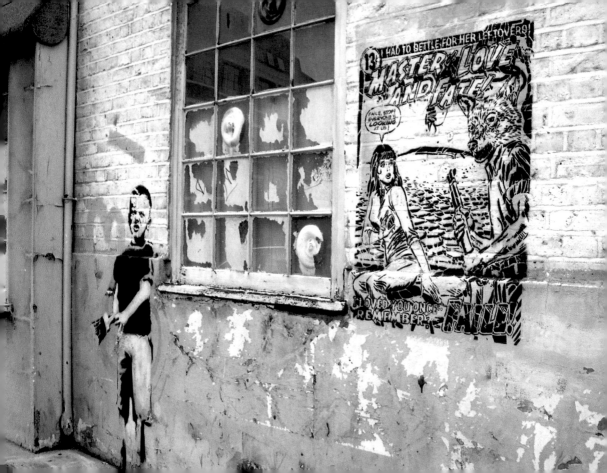

PAPA'RAT'ZI

Post Code - EC1R 0DY
Map / GPS reference - TQ 31494 82185

Location
Bottom end of Clerkenwell Close.

Strangely tucked away on the side of some flats where few will see this photographer-cum-rat.

Worth mentioning as the 'Banksy' tag is on backwards….. A little bit of alcohol can obviously make for a fun evening….

Status
Fading, but still there.

Next
Return to Clerkenwell Green, and walk down to the main road - Clerkenwell Rd (A5201).

BLT TIP
Banksy's 'Justice' statue was famously unveiled to a scrum of people on Clerkenwell Green in 2004. Nothing survives today though, not even an old pair of frilly knickers (unless you get lucky after Turnmills chucks out on a Friday night).

F9

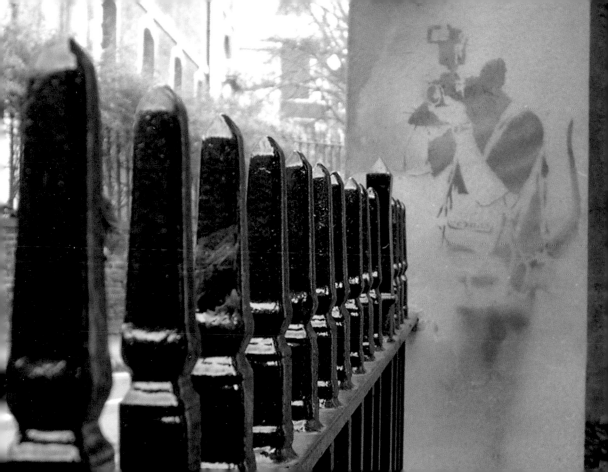

PENSIONER THUGS

('Thugs For Life' / 'Old Skool')
Post Code - EC1R 5DL
Map / GPS reference - TQ 31299 82030

Location
Clerkenwell Rd (A5201), near Saffron Hill.

This has had various incarnations (including the occasional tags of 'Thugs For Life' & 'Old Skool') but may not last long. It is now ominously behind bars awaiting redevelopment of the small car park it is part of. It shows Banksy's pensioner thugs with their B-Boy gear, zimmer frames and bling.The massive, and probably painstaking, stencils for this graffiti are shown at the end of the Wall & Piece book.

Status
Still there.

Next
Walk anyway you want to get to the Farringdon Rd (A201), but I would suggest using Back Hill (almost opposite Pensioner Thugs) because a newsagent there (Joys Cards & News, 3 Back Hill, EC1R 5EN) has a great shop shutter done by Mr P from London Frontline.
(check out www.londonfrontline.com)

F10

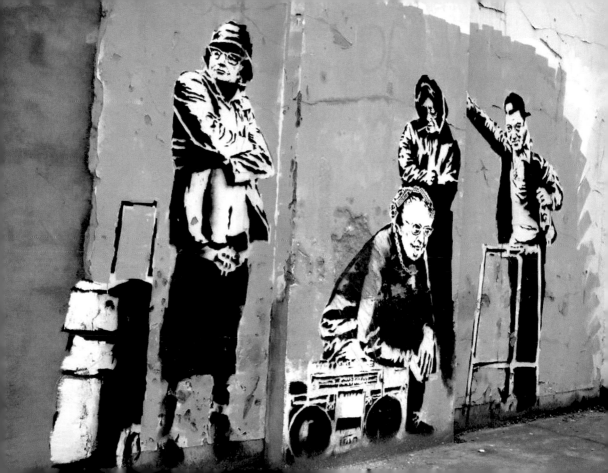

GANGSTA RAT

Post Code - EC1R 4QD
Map / GPS reference - TQ 31193 82422

Location
Roseberry Avenue (A401), very near the junction with Farringdon Rd (A201).

This was on the metal box of City News (4 Exmouth Market) but around October 2006 it was reported that the whole box was sold! A nice shiny new one replaced it. By November it was already being sold on eBay.

Status
Gone.

Next
Turn around and look over to the other side of the road to spot the cash machine.

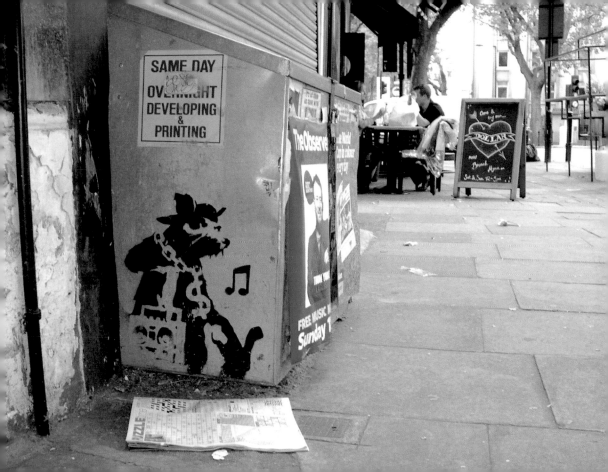

CASH MACHINE & GIRL

Post Code - WC1X 0DW
Map / GPS reference - TQ 31148 82454

Location
Roseberry Avenue (A401), very near the junction with Farringdon Rd (A201).

This is quite well known in London but strangely I can't find it in any books. It's a cash machine with a mechanical arm grabbing a girl. What on earth does this mean? Anyway, a long time ago this site started as just a rat on an old window. When the window was bricked up it then had the cash machine put on it, with Banksy / D*face's 'di-faced' tenners (£10 notes with Princess Di on them instead of the Queen) spewing out of it. Later, the arm and girl were added. Wasn't that history lesson interesting? I could have been a teacher; I would have loved to try the leather elbow patch & tweed look.

Status
Still there.

Next
Walk up Exmouth market.

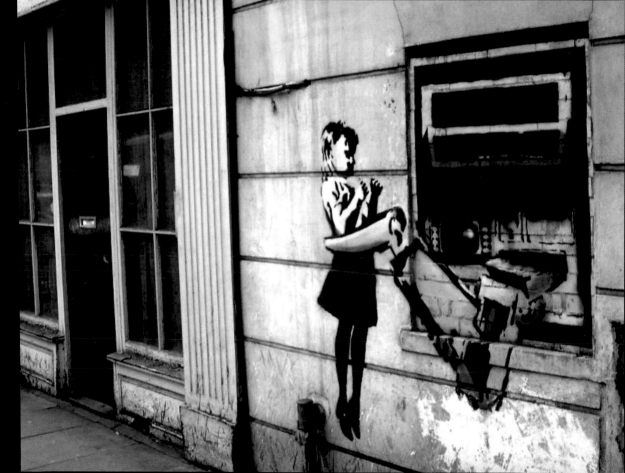

PAPA 'RAT' ZI RAT

Post Code - EC1R 4QL
Map / GPS reference - TQ 31296 82489

Location
On the entrance wall of the 'Movie World' shop, on Exmouth Market.

Another good example of the mutant photographer-cum-rat.

Status
Peeling, but acceptable. The wall seems to have been repainted, and they carefully painted around the Banksy ☺

Next
Return to the Farringdon Rd (A201) and continue past the enormous Mount Pleasant Post office site.

F15

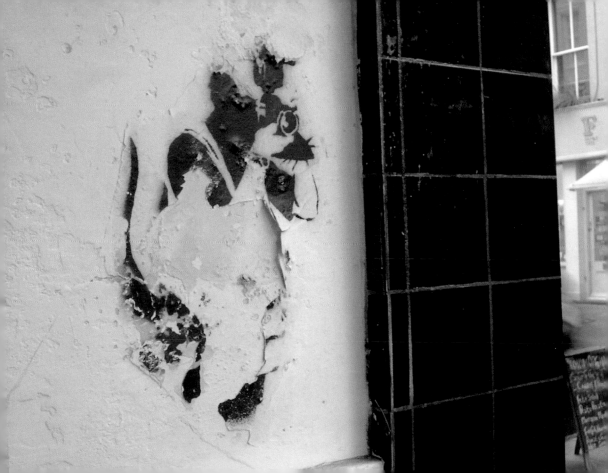

'Always Fail(e)'
Post Code - EC1R 3AS
Map / GPS reference - TQ 31011 82486

Location
By a bus stop on the Farringdon Rd (A201), near the junction with Calthorpe St.

This shows another example of Banksy's placard rat. It used to say 'Always Fail', but now reads 'Always Faile', which may or may not be a cheeky pun from the Faile crew!

Status
Faded but still there.

The end
It's a bit of a walk to either Angel, King's Cross or Farringdon tubes, or a number 53 bus towards either King's Cross or Farringdon.

F14

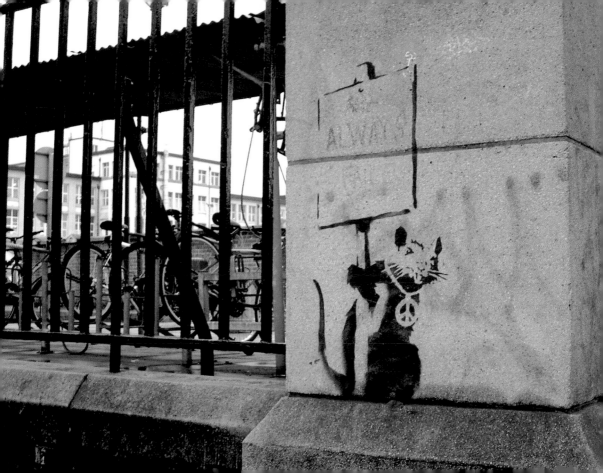

WATERLOO
SOUTH BANK
&
VICTORIA
EMBANKMENT
A.K.A.
THE RIVERSIDE
RAT TOUR...

iNTRODUCTiON

This tour goes around the Lower Marsh / Waterloo area, then all along the South Bank from the Mortar Rats (opposite the Houses of Parliament) to London Bridge, then crosses over the river to visit the ones on the North side of the river, finishing at Embankment tube station.

The route goes close to lots of tube stations (London Bridge, Monument, Bank, Cannon St, Blackfriars, Embankment, etc).

Although this is quite a long way, it's all pretty flat and as it doesn't involve any non-avoidable steps I would have thought that it could be done by someone using a wheelchair or a baby buggy.

You won't need a tube / bus / whatever ticket for this... it's just a lot of walking. When I did it as a tour it took over 2 ½ hours for the full tour. One section of the route can be missed out if you prefer a shorter walk (approx 2 hours).

START

A convenient starting point is Lambeth North Tube station (Bakerloo Line only). This station is pretty quiet, but is also walkable distance from Waterloo as well, which offers more tube interchanges (Jubilee, Waterloo and Northern lines) and national rail services.

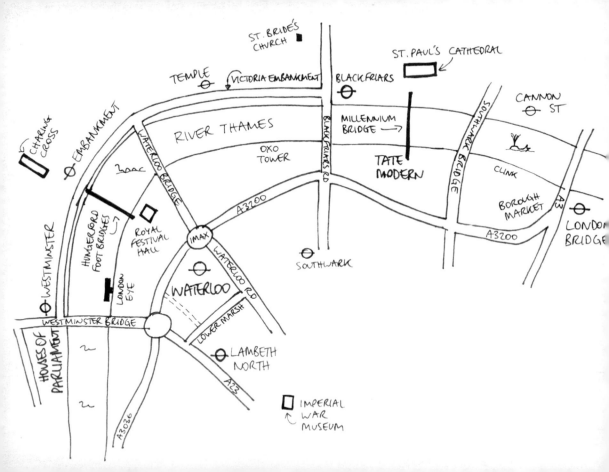

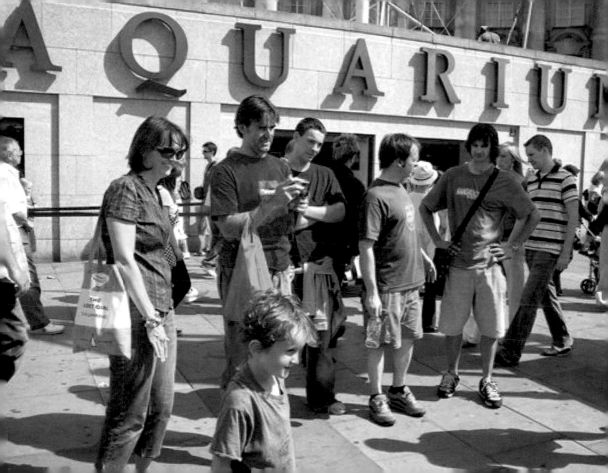

Post Code - SE1 7AB
Map / GPS reference - TQ 31209 79751

Location
Corner of Lower Marsh and Baylis Rd.

Directions
From Lambeth North Station - Turn right out of the station and walk down Baylis Rd.

From Waterloo Station - come out the Waterloo Rd exit. Turn right and walk down the Waterloo Rd (A301), to Baylis Rd and Lower Marsh.

It seems like Banksy blitzed the Lower Marsh area at some point. This is a rat piece I've not seen elsewhere; with a marker pen in its hand. This was on a telecoms metal box (always a favourite Banksy target!) but has now been buffed.

Status
Buffed.

Next
Continue up Lower Marsh.

R1

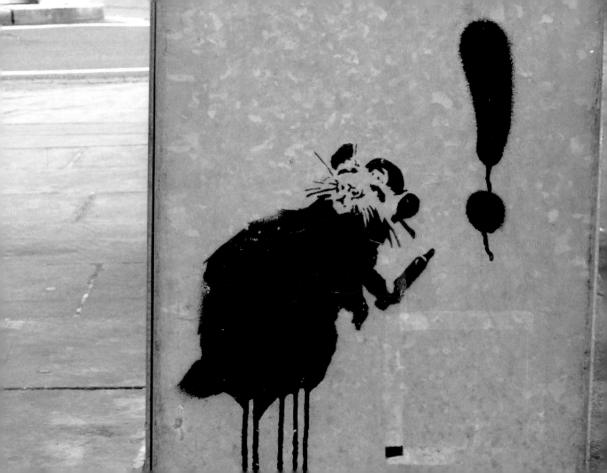

Post Code - SE1 7AB
Map / GPS reference - TQ 31161 79762

Location
On the metal box outside 'Supreme General Stores' on Lower Marsh.

On one of Banksy's favourite mediums... the metal boxes outside newsagent shops. Often partly obscured by posters.

Status
Still there.

Next
Continue up Lower Marsh, on the same side of the street.

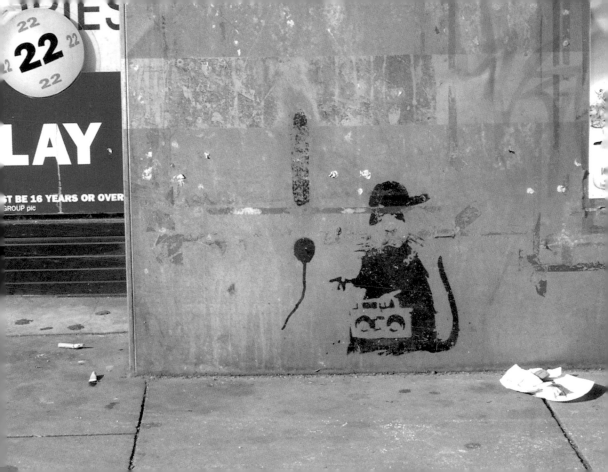

DESIGNATED PICNIC AREA

Post Code - SE1 7AD
Map / GPS reference - TQ 31070 79688

Location
On the side of a skanky alley about half way along Lower Marsh (next to 'Crockatt & Powell Booksellers')

Usually the arrow will invariably be pointing to some litter or rotting veg! Lower Marsh is still a very active & historic market area.

Status
So faded it might as well be considered buffed now.
(see inset photo)

Next
Continue up Lower Marsh, on the same side of the street.

R5

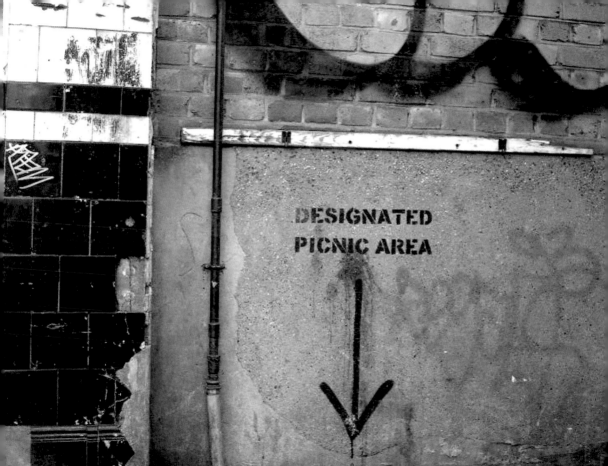

HELP ME RAT

Post Code - SE1 7AE
Map / GPS reference - TQ 31017 79637

Location
On the metal box outside a newsagent on Lower Marsh (opposite Ryman's).

This is a rat piece I've not seen elsewhere; a rat scrawling 'help me' on a newsagent's metal box (always a favourite Banksy target!).

Status
Still there, but the 'help me' phrase has been scrawled over.
(see inset photo)

Next
Turn around and return just a few metres down Lower Marsh, before taking the pedestrian walkway down to the underneath of Waterloo Station.

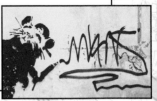

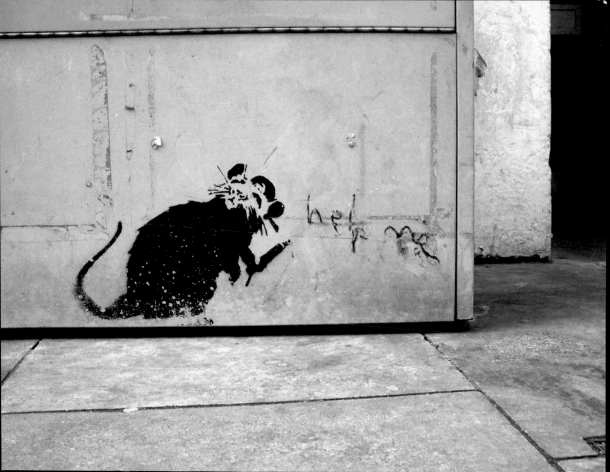

MONKEY DETONATOR

Post Code - SE1 7AE
Map / GPS reference - TQ 30997 79717

Location
In the tunnel underneath Waterloo Station (Leake St).

When I took a group on a tour of graffiti in Shoreditch, one comment was that, "I've never been in so many skanky alleys in my life". This Waterloo underpass is far more piss stained skanky, as a monkey detonates a bunch of bananas...

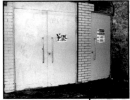

Status
I just revisited it (Oct 2006) and it has been painted over....

Next
Continue along the underpass, probably holding your nose by this point...

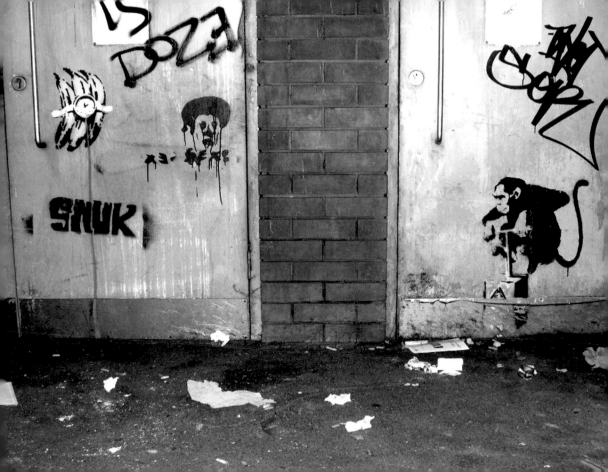

SNORTING COPPER

Post Code - SE1 7NN
Map / GPS reference - TQ 30890 79791

Location
Just out of the tunnel underneath Waterloo Station (Leake St).

Banksy's infamous Snorting Copper, now made rarer by being the only
surviving example since the Shoreditch (Location S18)
one was buffed.

Note the Space Invader above it.

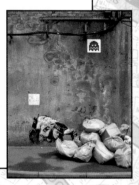

Status
Still there but it is visibly fading, especially the face
[the Space Invader above is still perfect].

Next
Continue to the main road (York Rd) and at the roundabout,
head for Westminster Bridge.

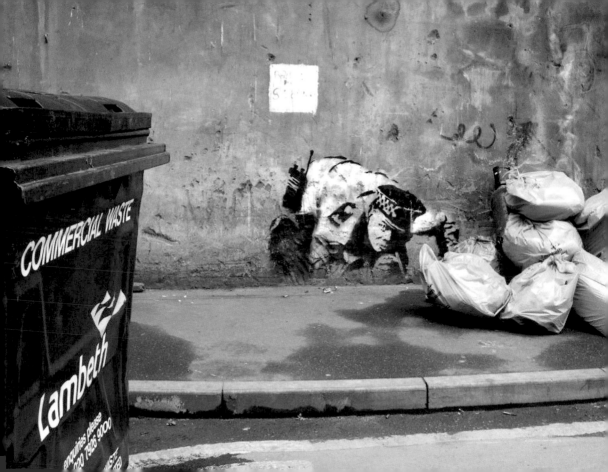

MORTAR RATS

Post Code - SE1 7NN
Map / GPS reference - TQ 30890 79791

Location
Two separate (but similar) examples, on the riverside granite blocks of the pedestrianised walk of the South Bank. One is close to Westminster Bridge. The other is several hundred metres further up, towards Lambeth Bridge.

The Houses of Parliament and 'Big Ben' can just be spotted, looming in the background, its assumed 'target'.

Banksy's tag is just visible in the corner of each. One has had some diving figures added to it; I doubt these are by Banksy as they seem to spoil the composition.

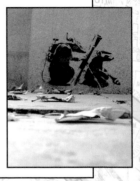

Status
Still there.

Next
Return to Westminster Bridge and walk under it (towards the London Eye).

R7

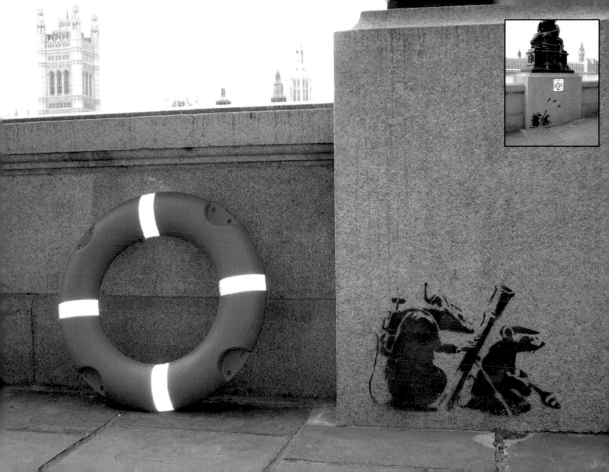

THIS IS NOT A
PHOTO OPPORTUNITY

Post Code - SE1 7JA
Map / GPS reference - TQ 30594 79812

Location
On the riverside granite blocks of the pedestrianised walk of the South Bank,
close to the London Eye (by the largest Dali Statue).

Possibly Banksy's most photographed stencil, as many people deliberately
or accidentally get their photos taken here (it overlooks over the Houses of
Parliament).

Status
Still there.

Next
Continue along the South Bank.

R8

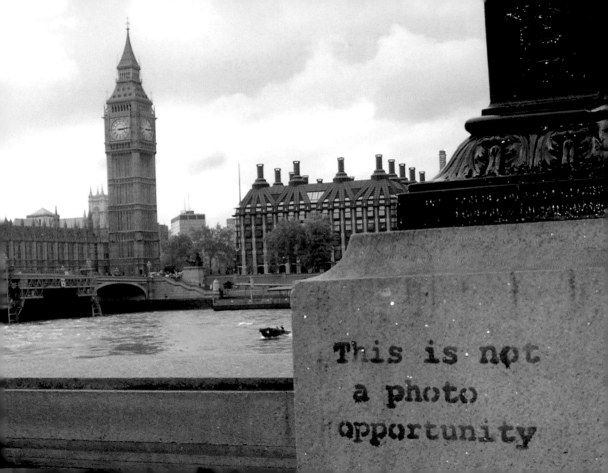

BLT tip

This area (R7 & R8) is a good area to spot the white line on the walkway.

This was a white line that stretched for a long way. It seems to start around the London Eye, and run along the south bank, over Lambeth road and around the houses to a bridge in Whitgift Street.

I think a snorting copper was at this end but there's nothing to be seen now...

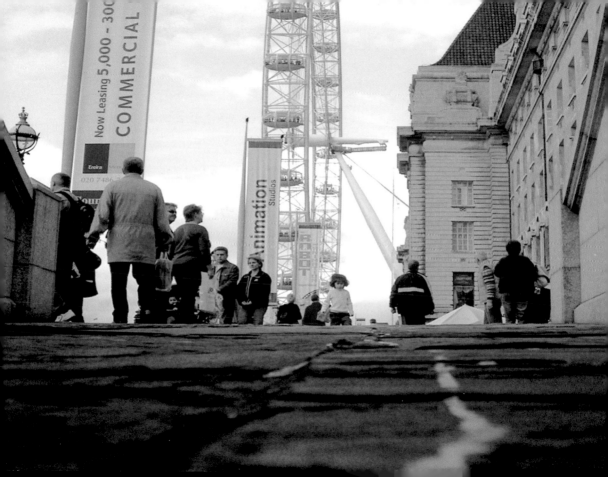

Post Code - SE1 7NN
Map / GPS reference - TQ 30890 79791

Location
On the riverside granite blocks of the pedestrianised walk of the South Bank, just before the Hungerford Footbridges.

A rare, slightly surviving sawing rat, complete with fag and beret. The circle on the pavement that accompanied these sawing rats has long gone though.

Status
Still there, but rather faded.

Next
Continue along the South Bank.

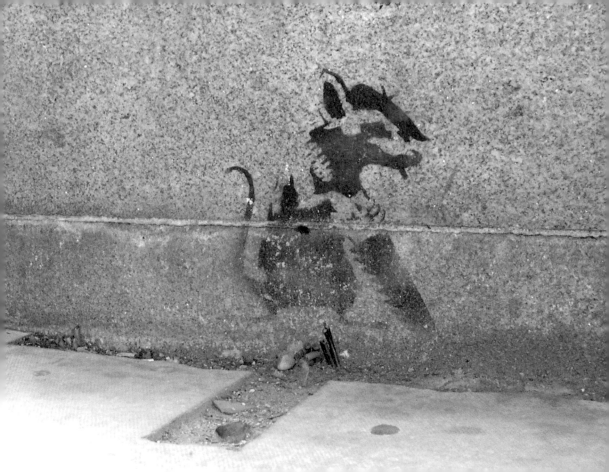

GANGSTA RAT

Post Code - SE1 8XZ
Map / GPS reference - TQ 30764 80331

Location
On the riverside granite blocks of the pedestrianised walk of the South Bank.
On the entrance to Festival Pier (opposite the Queen Elizabeth Hall).

Status
Still there but has been scrawled over with some
bubble graffiti.

Next
Continue along the South Bank.

BLT TIP
'BORING' was infamously
sprayed by Banksy, using a
modified fire extinguisher, in
massive red letters on the
Waterloo Bridge side of the
National Theatre.

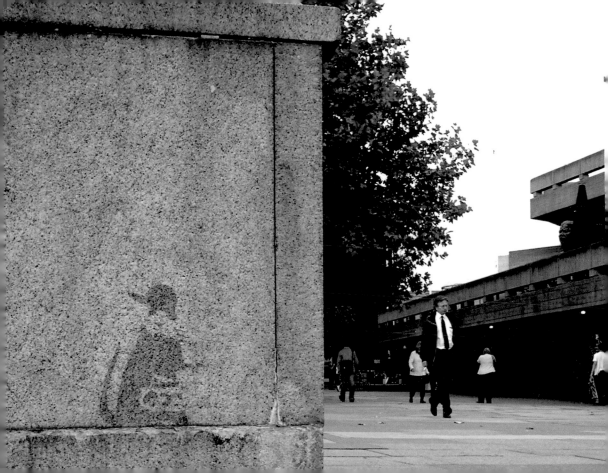

TINY SMILEY COPPER

Post Code - SE1 8TL
Map / GPS reference - TQ 30895 80427

Location
On the riverside granite blocks of the pedestrianised walk of the South Bank, just after Waterloo Bridge / Hungerford Footbridges.

This may or may not be a real Banksy. It is so small (and not seen elsewhere) and not great quality (not helped by the rough granite surface).

Status
Almost gone.

Next
Continue along the South Bank to the Tate Modern.

BLT TIP
There were two Girl With Balloon stencils along the South bank. Both have gone, but are still slightly visible. One was on the East side of Waterloo Bridge (by the National Theatre). The other was on the East side of Blackfriars Bridge. There were also a few 'Buried Treasures' but they have also virtually gone.

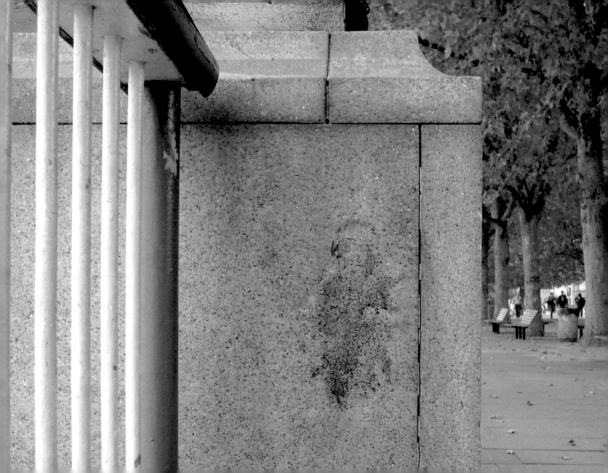

THIS IS NOT A
PHOTO OPPORTUNITY

Post Code - SE1 9TG
Map / GPS reference - TQ 31973 80541

Location
On a rusting old rubbish bin, on the pedestrianised walk of the South Bank,
right outside the Tate Modern.

Status
Still there.

Next
Continue along the South Bank, past the Clink
(where there used to be Banksy stuff) & Stoney Street,
and into Park St.

BLT TIP
For a shorter tour miss out R13
& 14 by crossing over the river
on the Millennium Foot bridge
(the 'wobbly' bridge) and con-
tinuing to R15.

R12

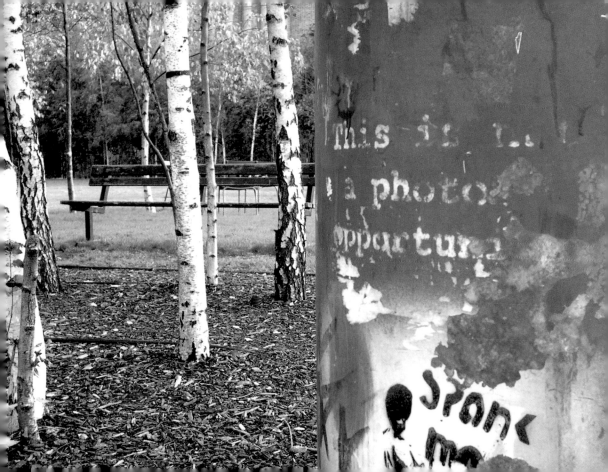

THIS IS NOT A PHOTO OPPORTUNITY

Post Code - SE1 9TG
Map / GPS reference - TQ 31973 80541

Location
On a lovely old building on Park Street, behind Borough Market.

This building was used as the hideaway in the film 'Lock Stock and Two Smoking Barrels'.

Status
Still there but someone has tried to scrub off the word 'not'.

Next
Go back to Borough Market, join Borough High St (A3) and head over London Bridge.

Go down to the riverside walk on the north side of the river. Walk westwards.

R15

BLT TIP
As you walk past the 'London Bridge Tandoori Restaurant' on the south side of London Bridge, you might recognise the advertising hoarding where Banksy scrawled 'The Joy of Not Being Sold Anything'. As show on a video on Banksy's site, and in the 'Pictures of Walls' book. Post Code - SE1 9QG / Map / GPS reference - TQ 32701 80267

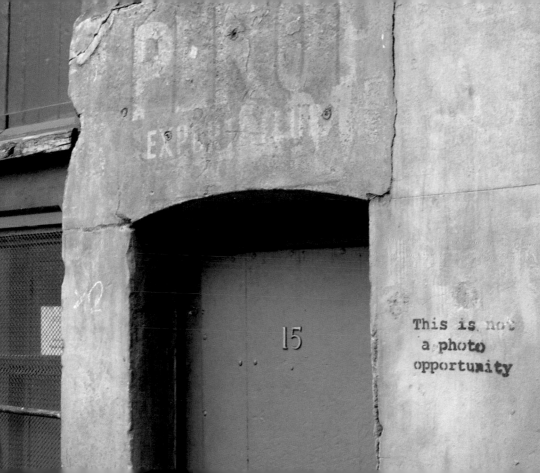

PLACARD RAT - YOU LOSE

Post Code - EC4R 3UE
Map / GPS reference - TQ 32586 80661

Location
At the riverside end of All Hallow's Lane (underneath Cannon St station).

This really sticks in my mind because when I first visited it I found a guy next to it, living in a cardboard box, with little except a radio & blanket. It felt really meaningless to take the photos, and also it could be demeaning to him. I talked with him for a long time, and asked 'permission' to take a photo of the wall (not getting him in the photo).

The irony of the placard 'message' dug home. This is just one reason I support The Big Issue, try to talk to people I meet rather than just pass them by, and try to help them a little.

Status
Still there, but the whole tunnel is being redeveloped.

Next
Continue along the riverside to Blackfriars (there are unfortunately a few bits on this side of the river where it isn't a riverside path as such, and you have to take detours inland).

> ### BLT TIP
> It is difficult to explain how to get to R15. A map and the use of the subways at Blackfriars station will help. You can obviously miss it out if you prefer.

R14

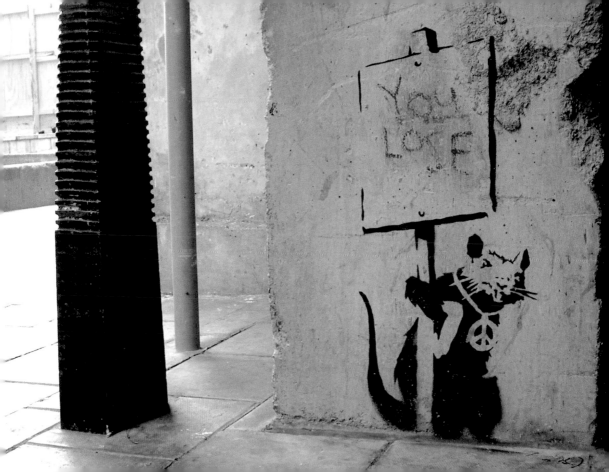

TOXiC RAT

Post Code - EC4Y 8AU
Map / GPS reference - TQ 31573 81134

Location
On the steps of a little passageway to St. Bride's Church. Just off Bride Lane.

Although this is not the greatest Toxic rat left in London, it is the one with the best setting, as it not only has St. Bride's Church (the famous 'Fleet St' church) in the background, but also cleverly uses the steps as if the rat is pouring the green waste down them.....

Status
Faded but still there.

Next
Return to the riverside as best you can.

R15

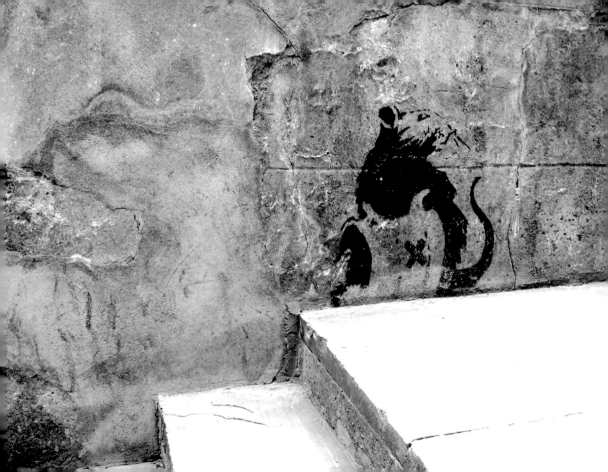

PHOTOGRAPHER RAT

Post Code - EC4Y 0HJ
Map / GPS reference - TQ 31320 80802

Location
On a metal utilities box on the Victoria Embankment (A3211), just after
Blackfriars (near the boat HMS President).

That's me that is. A photographer rat.

Again, this Banksy stencil seems to get given respect by others. Each time I
see it is has a different variety of stickers surrounding it, but they are always
around it rather than directly on it....

Status
Still there.

Next
Continue along the riverside (Victoria Embankment).

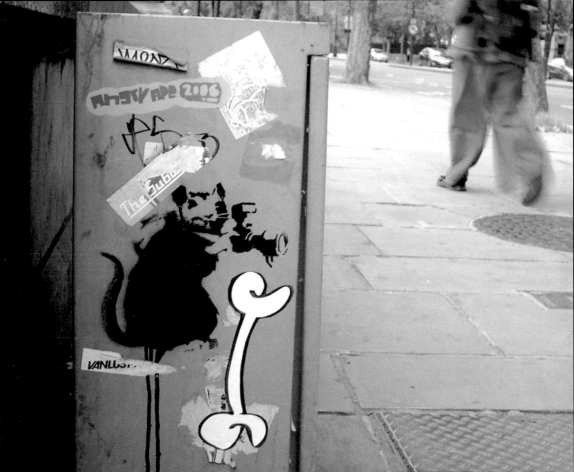

Post Code - WC2R 2PP
Map / GPS reference - TQ 31043 80786

Location
On the granite section of the riverside wall, near a memorial on the Victoria
Embankment (A3211). Near the boat HQS Wellington. Opposite Temple tube
station.

An excellent placard rat, with a big question mark on the placard. Still looks
really fresh despite being there for years.

Status
Still there.

Next
Continue along the riverside (Victoria Embankment).

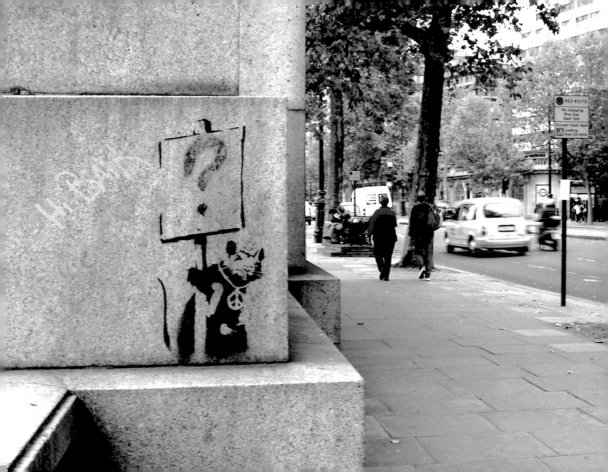

Post Code - EC4Y 0HJ
Map / GPS reference - TQ 31320 80802

Location
Above a green utilities box under Waterloo Bridge, on the corner of Savoy St

This was a very clean rat until rude, and frankly rather confused, graffiti was added close to it......something about polos and blow jobs....

Status
Still there

Next
Continue along the riverside (Victoria Embankment).

R18

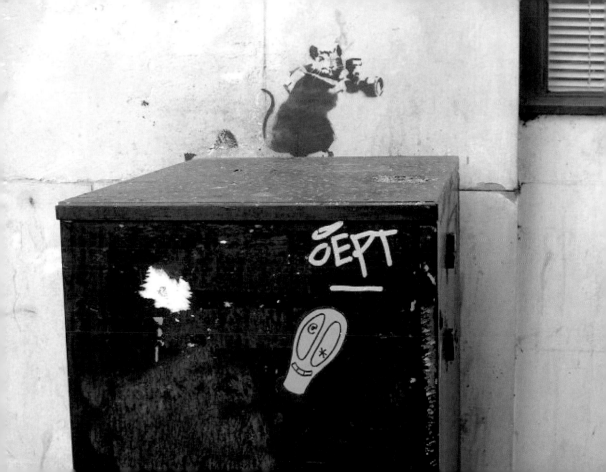

Post Code - WC2N 6NS
Map / GPS reference - TQ 30438 80323

Location
On the massive concrete struts of the Hungerford footbridge (east side). Opposite Embankment tube, on the Victoria Embankment (A3211).

Another 'Go Back To Bed' rat. Perfectly placed to catch commuters and early morning joggers, both of whom should know better.....

Status
Buffed in mid 2006.

The End
From this end point it is easy to get anywhere. Embankment tube is right in front of you, and it's a really easy walk to Charing Cross, Trafalgar Square or Waterloo.

R19

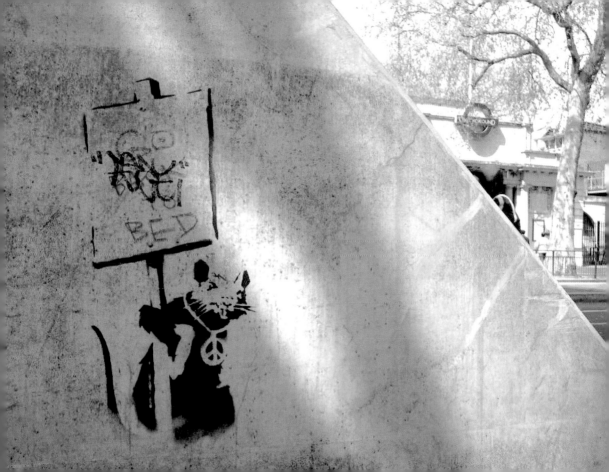

THANKS AND ACKNOWLEDGEMENTS

Obviously the real credit must go to all the artists who do their work on the street. Please support them. Links to their various websites etc are on the next pages.

The first, and main thanks has to be for Stef who asked me, in one of those Friday afternoon moments, if I had ever thought of making my tours and photos into anything more, such as a book (I had - great minds thinks alike eh? - but the book mapped out in my head was on Eine, not Banksy). He also pushed me all the way through the process, and did all of the painstaking graphic design and put up with my perfectionism.

The second thanks has to be for Sam, who handled all the print brokerage, helped me on the streets (no, he isn't actually my pimp…..although it may feel like it some times), generally encouraged me, and was always around for a chat and a wander.

Respect to Steve at 'Art of the State' and Tristan Manco.

And as mentioned at the start of the book, thanks to all the people who responded to my leading questions and annoyance of where to find a lot of this graffiti.

Although this book is in no way sanctioned by Pictures On Walls or The Big Issue, I greatly respect them both and give thanks to their work. Particular thanks to lovely Steph who used to work @ POW.

CREDITS

All photographs (bar two - see below) and text are by Martin Bull. Hand printed, limited editions of his black & white photos of graffiti are available via www.shellshockphotos.co.uk

Many thanks to Dave and Juliette for their photograph of the Shoreditch tour in September 2006 (shown just before location S17).

Many thanks to Sam for his photograph of the tour of Waterloo / South Bank in August 2006 (shown at the introduction to that section).

Many, many thanks for all the graphic design by Stef at Hoodacious - www.hoodacious.co.uk

LiNKS

Banksy - www.banksy.co.uk
Pictures On Walls (POW) - www.picturesonwalls.com
Faile - www.faile.net
Arofish - www.arofish.org.uk
D*face - www.dface.co.uk
Space Invader - www.space-invaders.com
Obey (Shepard Fairey) - www.obeygiant.com
Blek Le Rat - www.bleklerat.tk & http://blekmyvibe.free.fr
Art of the State - www.artofthestate.co.uk

The Mighty Gas - www.bristolrovers.co.uk
TU ink - www.tuink.co.uk
Pogo Café, Hackney - www.pogocafe.co.uk
The Big Issue - www.bigissue.co.uk
Hoodacious - www.hoodacious.co.uk
My own website - www.shellshockphotos.co.uk

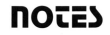

NOTES

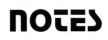

NOTES